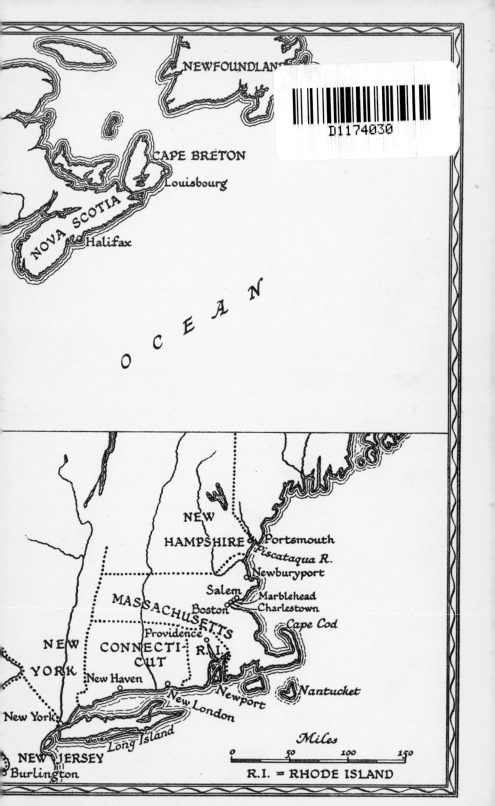

NEWFOUNDLAND

CAPE BRETON

Louisbourg

NOVA SCOTIA

Halifax

OCEAN

NEW
HAMPSHIRE
Portsmouth
Piscataqua R.
Newburyport
Salem
Marblehead
Charlestown
Boston
MASSACHUSETTS
Cape Cod

Providence
NEW
CONNECTI-
CUT
R.I.
YORK
New Haven
Newport
Nantucket
New London
New York
Long Island
NEW JERSEY
Burlington

Miles

0   50   100   150

R.I. = RHODE ISLAND

YANKEES
and
CREOLES

YANKEES and CREOLES

*The trade between
North America and
the West Indies before
the American Revolution*

RICHARD PARES
Fellow of All Souls College, Oxford

HARVARD UNIVERSITY PRESS
CAMBRIDGE, MASSACHUSETTS
1956

PRINTED IN GREAT BRITAIN

PREFACE

I COLLECTED the materials for this book more than twenty-five years ago on a visit to the United States and the West Indies. Thereafter I was distracted by other projects, then by the war, so that I never had time to use this material until lately. I should have expected that, during this quarter of a century of gestation, some historian in the United States would have published a book on a subject so important in early American history. But, from what I can find out, nobody appears to have thought of doing so. I therefore think it right to offer this book to the public, although it has some of the disadvantages which must result from so long an interval between conception and birth.

One of these disadvantages is the danger that, in the interval, some of the materials may have disappeared or, more likely, have been reclassified. I know that such a reclassification has taken place in the Brown MSS. at the John Carter Brown Library, since Professor James B. Hedges gives references, which did not exist in my time, in his book *The Browns of Providence Plantations*. The same thing may have happened elsewhere; if so, then my references may not be of much use in tracing the original manuscript. My health does not permit me to revisit the United States in order to give up-to-date references, but I think that it is better to give the indications which would have served to identify the documents in 1929, than to give none at all.

I should like to express my thanks, in the first place, to the Rockefeller Foundation, for awarding me the Fellowship which made this book possible. Also I should like to thank the owners of manuscripts and the Librarians of many institutions for their kindness, or that of their predecessors. In particular I wish to express my gratitude to the Essex Institute of Salem, Mass.; the Graduate School of Business Administration, Harvard

University; the Boston Public Library and the New England Historical and Genealogical Society of Boston, Mass.; Mr. John Nicholas Brown and the John Carter Brown Library, also the Rhode Island Historical Society of Providence, R.I.; the Newport Historical Society, Newport, R.I.; the New York Public Library and the New York Historical Society; the Historical Society of Pennsylvania and the Library Company of Philadelphia; the Library of Congress, Washington; and the Institute of Jamaica, Kingston, Jamaica.

My wife and my sister Elisabeth Humphreys have given me active help of many kinds in the preparation of the manuscript and the index. I am grateful to them both.

R.P.

CONTENTS

I. THE TRADERS

II. THE OUTWARD CARGOES

III. THE RETURN CARGOES

IV. THE WEST INDIA TRADE IN THE NORTH AMERICAN ECONOMY

CHAPTER I

THE TRADERS

I. WHO WERE THE ENTREPRENEURS?

HISTORIANS of the British Empire have long recognized the importance of the trade carried on before the American Revolution between North America and the West Indies. Without it the sugar colonies could not have existed and the North American colonies could not have developed. The balance between the tropical and temperate zones within the empire was a matter to be considered when peace treaties were negotiated;[1] and the preference for the West Indians over the North Americans which the imperial parliament showed, perhaps unfairly and injudiciously, in its legislation may have predisposed the latter to revolution.[2] But, although much has been written of this conflict of interests and its influence on policy, much less is known of the trade itself—of the way in which it was carried on. Nearly forty years ago Professor Herbert Bell wrote an excellent short article on the subject;[3] but perhaps a study of a somewhat longer period, drawn from a rather wider range of sources, may throw some new light on the people who conducted this trade, the purposes for which they conducted it, and the methods by which they did so.

The first founders of the English colonies did not distinctly mean to establish complementary sources of supply. They

---

[1] I refer especially to the so-called "Canada–Guadeloupe" controversy of 1760–2 (see W. L. Grant, in *American Historical Review*, xvii, 735–43, and C. W. Alvord, *The Mississippi Valley in British Politics* (Cleveland, 1917), i, 49–74). But I do not believe this controversy of pamphleteers had much effect upon the minds of British statesmen (see my book, *War and Trade in the West Indies* (Oxford, 1936), pp. 216–26).

[2] I refer to the Molasses Act of 1733 and the Sugar Act of 1764. Here, again, it is now generally held that the former and even the latter had much less to do with the Revolution than historians used to suppose. (See O. M. Dickerson, *The Navigation Acts and the American Revolution* (Philadelphia, 1951), pp. 82–7, 172–5.)

[3] *American Historical Review*, xxii (1917), 272–87.

knew what they wanted, and they mostly wanted the same
things—wine, oil, sugar, silk and other products of warm
climates for which the Englishman had (or so he thought) to
pay through the nose to foreigners. But they did not know
where they would ultimately find these things: thus, they would
have grown sugar in Virginia if they could have done so, and
they grew tobacco in Barbados before they found that sugar
would answer better. Only after some years of trial and error
did the familiar pattern of American trade become clear. The
colonies north of the Mason-Dixon line had few staples of any
value in the European markets but a permanent surplus of food
and lumber; the West Indies, just the contrary; and the hybrid
colonies from Maryland to Carolina produced both staple crops
and a less important surplus of certain kinds of food. This
differentiation of products first became important about 1640–
1650. The end of the immigration boom in New England must
have made food and lumber available for export, and forced
the colonists to find new methods of paying their debts in
England. About the same time the beginning of the sugar
boom in the West Indies increased purchasing-power and
accentuated the temptation to sacrifice food production to the
dominant cash crop.

The differentiation of products was obvious, for it created
the trade between North America and the West Indies. But
other differentiations were no less important.

In the first place, the two groups of societies differed more
and more from each other. It may seem obvious to us that this
must always have been so, but it was less obvious to the first
adventurers. There may have been puritan colonists who never
wished or hoped to found plantations (in the modern sense of
the word), but there was no necessary antithesis between puritanism and plantations: elements which, at any rate, passed
for puritan were strong in the early history of Virginia and
Jamaica, and the puritan syndicates interested in the tropical
colony of Old Providence and in the far from tropical colony of
Saybrook, Connecticut, had more than a little in common with
each other.[1] Some personal links between the northern and the

---

[1] A. P. Newton, *Colonising Activities of the English Puritans* (Yale, 1914), especially
chapter iii.

sugar colonies survived until the Revolution: the Redwoods of Newport, the Livingstons of New York and the Dickinsons of Philadelphia continued to hold West India property, and the descendants of other West Indian families—Searles, Silvesters and Morrises—lived in the northern colonies. The islands also contributed less valuable elements to the North American population, for their parochial poor relief often took the form of paying a passage for North America.[1] Visits were also exchanged by the sickly in search of health: Barbados sent Philadelphia her hard drinkers, with their 'carbuncled faces, slender legs and thighs, and large, prominent bellies',[2] and young Major George Washington accompanied his ailing brother in 1751–2 to Barbados, where he commented, with an emphasis surprising in a Virginian, on the planters' indebtedness.[3] But in spite of these feeble links, society developed on different lines in the West Indies and in North America.

The moral and religious aspect of this differentiation struck observers from the northern colonies more forcibly than any other. Politics and the chapter of accidents had helped to extinguish real puritanism in the West Indies, but it still flourished on the continent. As early as 1671 John Blackleach was shocked by the 'high presumptuous sinning' in Jamaica; Samuel Sewall feared that a young relative would lose his religion there, and the Quaker John Reynell left the island, after ten months, for this reason. But the puritans condemned more than the religion of Jamaica: they disliked the whole way of life. Isaac Norris tried to persuade his friend James Milles to leave it and come to Philadelphia, asking him to consider

whether the prospect of a little muck and that too (as times go) with fatigue and toil enough is of force sufficient to bury thee

---

[1] Until about 1720 the authorities of Boston rigorously warned out of the town those who arrived from the West Indies without any visible means of support, but they then became more lenient (see the Town and Selectmen's meetings in the *Reports of the Boston Record Commissioners*). Once, at least, they retaliated by shipping to Jamaica two free negroes who were 'old and likely in a short time to become a town charge' (*17th Report*, p. 88).

[2] So described by W. Sandiford, himself a Barbadian, in a letter of 30 May 1774 to James Pemberton (H[istorical] S[ocietyof] P[ennsylvania], Pemberton Papers, xxv, 76–7).

[3] *Daily Journal of Major George Washington in 1751–2*, ed. J. M. Toner (Albany, 1892), p. 59.

alive almost and perhaps at last dead too sooner than nature would demand her dues in a more temperate climate, prethee once more think of the vigorous sanity the Northwest gives us and look towards thy friends this way, tho' we do not live so flash and so fast yett wee live well and enjoy life with a better gust.[1]

There was a yet more important differentiation in the trade between the North Americans and the West Indians. The earliest documents on this trade—1640 to 1660—may be slightly misleading, just because they are legal records or, at least, enforceable contracts;[2] the trade may not always have been characterized by such stilted legality—indeed, the letter-book of Peleg Sanford, a nearly contemporary document, shows little sign of it.[3] But these records disclose unmistakably, along with other more familiar features, a state of affairs which was uncommon a century later.

In the first place, London merchants played an important part in the trade between New England and the West Indies. Many of the ships were theirs—naturally, since shipbuilding was only beginning in America. Their agents or contractors in Boston or Salem provided cargoes which were shipped at their risk to the West Indies and there sold on their account.[4] Secondly, the West Indians themselves were still active commercially and, to some degree, independent of the Londoners. The ships and cargoes in the trade between Boston and Barbados might almost as often belong to Barbadians as to Bostonians—there might even be some doubt whether a particular merchant was to be reckoned a Barbadian or a Bostonian. Indeed, Barbados was probably the more important mercantile centre of the two: more than once, New Englanders found that they could buy an assortment of goods for the slave trade

[1] John Blackleach to John Winthrop, October 1671, *Winthrop Papers* (*Mass*[*achusetts*] *H*[*istorical*] *S*[*ociety*] *Collections*, 4th series, vii), pp. 52–3; *Letter-Books of Samuel Sewall*, i, 83, 117; Isaac Norris to James Milles, 22 November 1703, H.S.P., Norris Letter-Book, ii, 111.

[2] *Suffolk Deeds* (14 vols., Boston, 1880–1902); *Aspinwall Notarial Record* (Boston, 1903); *Essex County, Records and Files of the Quarterly Court*, vols. i to v (Salem, 1912–1916); *Records of the Court of Assistants, Massachusetts Bay*, vols. ii to iii (Boston, 1901–28).

[3] Published by the Rhode Island Historical Society, 1928.

[4] *Suffolk Deeds*, i, 5, 12, 203; *Aspinwall Notarial Records*, pp. 255, 356; *Winthrop Papers* (*Mass. H.S. Collections*, 4th series, vi), p. 70.

at Barbados when they could not do so at home.[1] The financial independence of the West Indians had yet another effect. The New Englanders had already begun to think of their exports to the West Indies as a means of discharging their debts in England,[2] but the manner of doing so was not yet stereotyped as in the eighteenth century: buying a planter's bill of exchange on his London correspondent was only one way of doing it, for Barbados produce was as good as ready money in Barbados, in London, in Holland, or in Boston itself, whence it was often exported as a remittance to England before the Plantation Duties were imposed in 1673. Thus the independent planter and the independent merchant in the West Indies made the two American points of the triangle of trade almost equal to each other in importance, though neither of them could rival the European end.

These conditions changed, though the change was neither immediate nor complete. ⟨The goods and even the ships of the English merchants were still to be found, on occasion, in the eighteenth-century trade between the northern colonies and the West Indies.⟩ They were particularly evident in the early history of Pennsylvania, for the first Pennsylvanians, like the first New Englanders, were fresh from Europe and still supported by English capital, or at least, linked with it; some, like James Claypoole, had themselves been merchants in London before they were merchants in Philadelphia. The business papers of Isaac Norris (*ca* 1690–1710) contain many letters from his London correspondents instructing or at least allowing him to return their effects by shipping to Barbados or to Jamaica on their account; and he paid his own debts, e.g. for a clock, by the same method. When the *George* arrived in Jamaica from Philadelphia (some time in 1699) at least three of the eight owners of goods on board of her were English merchants—two in Bristol, one in London.[3]

The papers of John Reynell, a Philadelphia merchant of a later generation (*ca* 1730–60), reveal a variety of reasons why

---

[1] *Aspinwall Notarial Records*, pp. 220, 300.
[2] *Ibid.*, pp. 225, 287, 340; *Suffolk Deeds*, i, 271; ii, 133; iv, 35.
[3] Ledger of James Logan, 1699, H.S.P.

the merchants of England should engage in this trade. Reynell was a young man of no fortune, and some business men in Plymouth and Exeter seem to have consigned goods to him as a factor out of friendship (one of them said 'I can have no other inducement to continue a trade to Philad^a than to befriend thee.').[1] Like other beginners, he found it difficult to return his friends' effects direct to England, and propounded elaborate schemes for remitting via Jamaica, where one, at least, of his correspondents had relations or friends who could not only take charge of the cargoes but give him the necessary advice about markets.[2] He also encouraged the ship-owners among his acquaintance to send their vessels, or even to have vessels built in Philadelphia, assuring them blithely that there ought to be no difficulty in procuring freights to the West Indies and thence back to Philadelphia or home to England.[3] Yet those who took his advice were often disappointed. One of them wrote to him, 'The making remittances round by Antego and Jamaica will take up so much time, that a man will hardly see his money again returned in less than two years and upwards from the time of sending it out.'[4] Those who sent ships to Philadelphia with this purpose often regretted it, for no freight was to be had after all, and they had to fill up on their own account.[5]

Reynell himself began to sing a different tune, as he came to depend less on his factor's commissions. In September 1737 he was 'of opinion that according to the generall run of the Jamaica trade from here, you will hardly find it worth while, to send vessels here to load with bills of exchange, and to send 'em here to look for a freight, is sending of 'em on great uncertaintys.' In fact, he had ceased to see much point in the triangular trade as a means of paying for Philadelphia's imports from Great Britain. It might still be useful to those British merchants who, for their own reasons, wanted to make

[1] M. L. Dicker to J. Reynell, 9 September 1730, Reynell Papers, Box i, H.S.P.

[2] J. Reynell to M. L. Dicker, 19 June 1731, Reynell Letter-Book A, H.S.P.

[3] J. Reynell to Richard Deeble, 19 June 1731, 17 November 1733, *ibid.*, pp. 26, 77.

[4] M. L. Dicker to J. Reynell, 24 December 1730, Reynell Papers, Box i, H.S.P.; Peter and John Williams to J. Reynell, 1 December 1730, *ibid.*

[5] J. Reynell to Richard Deeble, 9 May, 17 July 1732, 29 May 1734, Reynell Letter-Book A, pp. 42, 48, 82.

sure of providing North American produce in the West Indies. Even here, it was clogged with disadvantages:

> The dry goods trade is grown very discouraging owing to the importing too large quantitys, which makes 'em sell lower and slower then they have done in times past, then the abominable long credit taken by our shopkeepers, is a very great hindrance to trade, but notwithstanding all these obsticles, do think that the carrying on a trade to any advantage from here to Jamaica must be done that way, and if you fall into that method you must always take care, to have your goods here 9 or 12 months before you expect your remittances to be made.[1]

Some of Reynell's English friends continued to use the triangular trade via Philadelphia and the West Indies; among them Michael Atkins, the recipient of the piece of advice I have just quoted. But he had a particular reason for doing so: he had a regular ship in the Jamaica trade and settled connexions with Jamaica planters, whom he wished to oblige by assuring their supplies of North American lumber. If he could have timed his ships so as to reach Jamaica by the end of December, it would have suited him to collect the lumber in this way. But he found by repeated experience that a ship which received her discharge in Bristol in August could not keep to this timetable, and lost her chance of a freight in Jamaica.[2] For this cause many promising schemes of triangular trade miscarried. British-owned vessels continued to appear in the trade between the continent and the colonies; but most of these were regular ships in the trade between Europe and the West Indies, which had been disappointed of a freight home by short crops in the islands, or had a few months to fill up because they had, for some reason, defaulted on their own time-table. Even visits of this kind were unusual. In the papers of Messrs. Lascelles and Maxwell, a London House trading to Barbados, projects were often discussed for sending the regular ships from the island to the continent in the off-season; but only once in thirty years

[1] J. Reynell to Michael Atkins, 29 September 1737, Reynell Letter-Book B, p. 22.

[2] Michael Atkins to J. Reynell, 23 February 1749/50, 10 April 1752, 15 January and 8 October 1755, Reynell Papers, Boxes v, ix, H.S.P.

was such a project executed, and the results were disastrous, for the vessel returned to Barbados too late in the season to get a full freight home. Some of these occasional visitors to the continent offered to carry goods on freight to the islands. Other British ship-owners in this predicament tried to trade on their own account; but they did so at a disadvantage: as Reynell's friend Atkins expressed it, 'Traders at the Northern Colonies have all the West India business to themselves, Europeans can have no encouragement for mixing with them in the comodities of provisions and lumber. You time things better than we and go to markett cheaper.'[1]

Not only had the British merchant almost disappeared from this trade; but the North American and West Indian merchants no longer shared the active part of it equally. Partnerships between West Indians and North Americans were not unheard of. Between 1726 and 1776, 82 vessels, mostly built at Philadelphia, were registered at that port as owned jointly by Pennsylvanians and West Indians.[2] Some North Americans, especially beginners and small traders, liked to have West Indian partners 'for dispatch sake', as Isaac Norris put it—by which he meant that the West Indian partner could buy produce at the best season and advance part of the ship's return cargo for North America before her outward cargo was all sold.[3] Not many partnerships of this sort have come to light, and very few permanent. There are some traces of West

[1] Michael Atkins to John Reynell, July 1751, *ibid.*, Box vi. Professor O. M. Dickerson (*The Navigation Acts and the American Revolution*, pp. 23–4) suggests a special reason why vessels owned in England could not carry West India produce from the islands to the continent: they were obliged, unlike vessels owned in the colonies, to give bond to land any goods enumerated under the Acts of Trade in Great Britain and nowhere else. This may be so; but I do not remember seeing the point mentioned in the correspondence of merchants; and it would not have affected the carriage of goods from the continent to the islands, since hardly any of the commodities in that trade were on the 'enumerated list'. This was the form in which British ship-owners were likely to concern themselves with the triangular trade, since they wanted to have their vessels in the islands to carry a cargo of sugar to Europe.

[2] As well as 49 others owned by West Indians alone or in partnership with merchants in Great Britain or the wine islands (*Pennsylvania Magazine of History and Biography*, vols. xxiii to xxviii).

[3] Isaac Norris to Richard Poor, Barbados, 13 December 1699, 5 April 1700; to Abraham Johns, 26 July 1700; to Richard Sleigh, Jamaica, 11 September 1701, Isaac Norris Letter-Books, i, 117, 161, 211, 345, H.S.P.

Indian ventures to North American ports; but they were few and, for the most part, small.[1]

The exceptions to this rule are of two kinds. On the one hand some of the big 'town agents' of Barbados and Jamaica occasionally thought it worth while to trade to North America on their own account. They may have belonged to the rising class of merchant-attorneys for absentee planters; at any rate, they had a constant demand for lumber and some responsibility for keeping the plantations supplied with this necessary article without which not a barrel of sugar or rum could be shipped. These people, such as Samuel Dicker, or Bayly, Elworthy and Bayly, of Kingston, Jamaica, or Alexander Sandiford of Bridgetown, Barbados, sometimes thought it worth while to contract for their lumber and provisions beforehand, and to get it brought to them by fixing a vessel in the trade (perhaps in partnership with a North American) or by promising a full freight of sugar home to a London ship if she would bring the lumber from the continent by such and such a date. But these schemes seldom lasted long; the merchant in the West Indies may have been glad enough to make sure of his lumber in a dear year, but as soon as the prices fell to the normal level or below it, he repented of his contract.[2]

The only other sign of independent trading activity comes from the French colonies in the West Indies. The business papers of Peter Faneuil of Boston present a very different picture from those of his contemporaries:[3] he seems to have been a factor rather than (or at least as much as) an independent merchant and the correspondents on whose cargoes he earned his largest commissions were Frenchmen. These French cargoes sometimes arrived in French shipping. It was not an easy trade to carry on. The admission of foreign vessels was held to be contrary to the Acts of Navigation, and they ran

[1] Mr. Byron Fairchild has called attention to a partnership of this sort between merchants at Barbados and Piscataqua in *Messrs. William Pepperrell* (Ithaca, 1954), p. 36.

[2] Samuel Dicker to J. Reynell, 27 April 1741; Bayly, Elworthy and Bayly to J. Reynell, 13 April, 25 May, 3 June, 10 October 1754, Reynell Papers, Boxes iii, viii, H.S.P.; Ezekiel Edwards to James Pemberton, 17 October 1772, Alexander Sandiford and Son to Pemberton and Edwards, 11 September 1773, Pemberton Papers, vols. xxiv and xxv, H.S.P.

[3] Preserved in the New England Historical and Genealogical Society, Boston.

some danger of getting themselves 'confisticated'. In fact, that
is what happened to a sloop with which Peter Faneuil was connected, and he could only argue that though she might have
been bound for Boston she never arrived there, having been
cast away, and 'a person is not to be hanged for design'.[1] One
might insure against risks of this sort by providing the ship with
double papers—a particularly easy thing when she was New
England built—and by putting two alternative masters, English
and French, in command of her.[2] But even then, the merchants
of Boston, so ready to trade with the French colonies on their
own account, might conceive a jealousy of the Frenchmen who
tried to assume an active part in this trade, and stir up the port
officials against them.[3] In general, it was a messy business,
chiefly recommended by the consideration that a French ship,
unlike an English one at that date, would have little or no
difficulty in getting herself admitted to the ports of the French
colonies. When the French authorities, in their greater and
greater need of North American produce, removed or reduced
the impediments to the admission of traders from the British
colonies, the chief incentive to French enterprise in this trade
disappeared.

Sometimes Peter Faneuil took to himself the entire cargoes of
these Frenchmen—i.e. he bought them, resold them in Boston
or shipped them coastwise and gave credit for them.[4] For
some, moreover, of these Frenchmen he was, in the long run,
decidedly in advance, that is, he habitually shipped their return
cargoes before he was in cash for what he had received. He also
shipped ventures of his own to the West Indies, sometimes consigning them to the same Frenchmen who had consigned their

---

[1] Peter Faneuil to Pierre du Cangé, 2 August 1738; to Jacques Casteia, 11
October 1738, Letter-Book of Peter Faneuil, *ibid.*

[2] For a French ship with two masters in this trade see Peter Faneuil's letter to
Louis Maitre, Cap Français, 11 December 1738, *ibid.* Collusive sales of British
colony built ships are described in a letter of Robert Dinwiddie, 17 March 1729/30,
Calendar of State Papers, America and West Indies, 1730, No. 121.

[3] Such an incident at Boston in 1718 is described in a letter of James Smith to
Josiah Burchett, 8 December 1718, in Richard West's 'Plantation Reports',
Library of Congress, pp. 60–2.

[4] This is indicated whenever an invoice of goods from a French merchant is
creditor in his ledger by 'Generall wares'. On occasions a whole cargo was disposed of in this way (e.g. on fo. 175 of his ledger).

cargoes to him. But these things were exceptional and do not conceal the fact that he normally acted as an agent; it looks as if the merchants of the French sugar colonies generally showed more enterprise and took more risks in this trade than those of the British.

Why were the merchants resident in the British sugar colonies so seldom active in this trade? The causes lie deep. At some time, probably about 1680 to 1700, the whole financial relation between the British sugar colonies and the mother country had changed.[1] The planters, tied by debt and the Navigation Acts to their London correspondents, had lost their independence and, as a result of this loss, had got into the habit of ordering their stores from London or Bristol, instead of buying for ready money on the spot; their produce had ceased to be ready money, had ceased to count as currency except for the payment of small debts, and had become a mere means of obtaining bills of exchange upon London. In consequence, the local merchants too had lost their active status. There were still many small firms of wholesalers or storekeepers, dealing largely in the produce of North America. But their attitude was passive for the most part: they sold, for a commission, the cargoes consigned to them by the merchants of North America or offered by transient captains of North American vessels. They could be pretty sure that these cargoes would come, without any contracts or any other positive action to attract them, for the produce of North America overflowed in all directions after 1715, and sellers' competition was always strong enough to bring it to their doors. Only the merchants of Kingston, Jamaica, traded largely on their own account, to the Spanish settlements. In the other British sugar islands it is very seldom that we hear of a merchant who, like Thomas Kerby of Antigua, traded with a sloop of his own to the northern colonies and expected those North American merchants for whom he sold goods on commission to do the same for him in return. But in the French sugar colonies, especially Martinique, the relation of the planters to the European capitalist was still, in the

---

[1] This change has been discussed briefly in a suggestive article by Mr. K. G. Davies (*Trans. Royal Historical Society*, 5th series, ii, 89–108), but a fuller treatment is necessary before the matter can be cleared up.

eighteenth century, more like what it had been at Barbados in
the seventeenth; and, as a corollary, the merchants of Martinique—the *commissionnaires*, as they were called—remained a
powerful and active class.[1] That is why they, and some of their
counterparts in St. Domingue, continued to consign produce
to Boston and to order return cargoes, on their own account,
as late as 1735.

The North Americans, then, were, for the most part, the
active elements in this trade; but what North Americans? To
answer this question would be to describe the specialization of
the merchant class (so far as it ever was specialized before the
Revolution). It appears likely that much of this business was,
from the beginning, in the hands of professional merchants; but
'returns via the West Indies' were the easiest of all games to
play, and there is some evidence that other classes of people—
for instance, officials and widows—occasionally played it on
a small scale. Even the business men themselves often played
it on a very small scale indeed: the ledgers of William Trent and
Pentecost Teague, for example,[2] show numerous little shipments, mostly of bread and flour. Such small shippers were
very often beginners; but Timothy Orne of Salem continued to
ship, alone or as a member of constantly fluctuating partnerships, quite small parcels until the end of his career. One might
think that this fragmentation was habitual in Salem, the home
of a fishing industry conducted on a system of very small shares;
but Richard Derby, likewise of Salem, graduated to big
business as Timothy Orne never did. Most of the merchants
whose papers survive, not only did much business, but relatively
big business with the West Indies. Perhaps, if the papers of the
small dealers had survived more abundantly, we should see
that amateurs continued to play an important part in this
trade; but I doubt it.

Very few of the great shippers of goods to the West Indies
were producers. The spermaceti candle manufacturers,

traders + producers

---

[1] For an account of these *commissionnaires*, see L. Ph. May, *Histoire Économique de
la Martinique* (Paris, 1930), pp. 208–11; M. Satineau, *Histoire de la Guadeloupe sous
l'Ancien Régime* (Paris, 1928), pp. 212–16. The *commissionnaires* seem to have
resembled the Barbados 'town agents'. For Thomas Kerby of Antigua, see Byron
Fairchild, *op. cit.*, pp. 54–5, 110–11.

[2] Preserved in the Historical Society of Pennsylvania.

especially the Browns of Providence, Rhode Island, shipped quantities of candles of their own make; but they also sold them in the home market, and on one occasion their supercargo in Surinam found himself undersold by their own customers.[1] The Browns also shipped their own iron to the West Indies, and so did one or two other owners of furnaces or forges; but, with these exceptions, the combination of producer and West India merchant was uncommon.[2] Most shippers to the West Indies bought the goods they shipped, or received them in pay for other goods. This is evident from the frequency with which they declined a particular bargain or branch of trade (or even, for the time being, all trade) as unprofitable. They would not have done so if they had had goods of their own produce which had to be sold at any cost.

The specialization of the merchants in this trade went hand in hand with another development—the increasing identification of the merchant with the ship-owner. This process was never by any means complete; but it seems to me that the earlier merchants were more often content to take freight on the ships of others, whereas their successors mostly possessed their own shipping.

The first shippers of all sometimes found a Dutch vessel put up on freight for the West Indies, before the Navigation Acts excluded these universal tramps from the English colonies.[3] After this resource was denied them, the shippers still found, for a time, plenty of space on the vessels of other merchants in their own ports, an occasional 'seeker' from England, or a Bermudian. (Some people preferred Bermudian vessels to any others, though others execrated the misbehaviour of their

---

[1] Simon Smith to Nicholas Brown and Co., 16 April 1769, papers of the Brigantine *Sally*, J[ohn] [Carter] B[rown] L[ibrary]. (It is evident from the documentation of Professor James B. Hedges's *The Browns of Providence Plantations* (Cambridge, Mass., 1952) that the Browns' papers have been classified since I saw them; but I cannot give the up-to-date references.)

[2] John Reynell once wrote, 'the purchasing of any merchant was not of any advantage to the merch^t for that he himself was obliged to purchase it with ready money and that the persons of whom it must be purchased were such as hardly ever shipt anything abroad' (J. Reynell to Michael Atkins, 29 September 1737, Reynell Letter-Book B, p. 22, H.S.P.).

[3] There are charter parties of Dutch vessels on pp. 83 and 215 of the *Aspinwall Notarial Records*, besides other references to a ship called the 'St. Martin of Allickemore', which I take to be Alkmaar.

captains.)[1] An importer or an exporter who was content to use these facilities could instruct his correspondent to 'send me some thing in every vessell that is bound for this place', and such a plan had its advantages, for it ironed out the fluctuations of markets at home and abroad though it diminished the chance of a 'great hit'.[2] Not that a conveyance offered every week or even every month: although little vessels were scuttling across the seas in all directions, a direct voyage between a minor island and a minor continental port might be infrequent. (Samuel Winthrop complained in 1663 that he had tried in vain for fifteen months to ship some effects from Antigua to Connecticut.[3])

But generally, after the middle of the eighteenth century, the freighters of goods in other people's vessels were the exception rather than the rule. There were more ships than freight for them, especially at the islands;[4] many captains whom their owners had instructed to get West India produce on freight had to wait months for it, or sail in ballast, or fill up on the owners' account.[5] Even in the home ports freight might be scarce, or confined to lumber which was less profitable than cask goods and, perhaps, only a paying proposition on big ships.[6] The owners might be very glad to carry stores for the

---

[1] Isaac Norris to Delaval and Carpenter, 16 August 1693, Norris Papers, i, 47, H.S.P.; John Watkins to Thomas Clifford, 15 June 1761, Clifford Correspondence, iii, no. 311, H.S.P.

[2] *Letter-Book of Peleg Sanford*, p. 10; G. G. Beekman to Kortright and Lawrence, 14 April 1756, Letter-Book of G. G. Beekman, N[ew] Y[ork] H[istorical] S[ociety]; Henry Bonnin to J. Reynell, 31 May 1731, Reynell Papers, Box i, H.S.P.

[3] *Winthrop Papers* (*Mass. H.S. Collections*, 5th series, viii), p. 251. Creditors in North America sometimes refused to believe this story (*Letter-Books of Samuel Sewall*, i, 108).

[4] This would depend on the assortment of the return cargo, a subject I shall have to discuss later. In general, a homeward cargo from the West Indies would be less bulky in proportion to its value than the outward cargo, unless it consisted of molasses; and even then it might be so, if molasses was dear then and there. This is why we hear more of vessels wanting freight at the islands than in North America.

[5] According to Captain Donnell, ships had lain five or six months at Antigua in 1754, the year of a very short crop, and were now going away in ballast. He may have been referring to English ships, for whom this would not be an unusual experience, but I rather think not. (N. Donnell to J. Reynell, 11 May 1754, Reynell Papers, Box viii, H.S.P.)

[6] Jonathan Dickinson to Isaac Gale, 28 April 1718, 6 July 1720, Letter-Book of Jonathan Dickinson, pp. 186, 327, L[ibrary] C[ompany of] P[hiladelphia], Ridgway Branch.

victuallers to the navy, who were sometimes the only people who had any freight to offer.[1] On the other hand, ship-owning had its advantages in this trade: the owner had at least the chance to decide whether to use his vessel for his own goods or to let her out to others; and, of course, he would use her himself if he thought well of the markets, whereas, if he did not, he would hope to find some shipper or charterer who was so ill-advised as to judge differently from himself.[2] The power of making this choice was probably worth much to him. He might, of course, compromise by filling her partly with his own goods, partly with those of others; owners often instructed their captains to do this, in one form or other.[3] But this had its disadvantages if he wished to get the top of the market, for the freighters might ship goods of the same kind as his own agents did, and lower the selling prices for him by their competition.[4] On the whole, therefore, many traders avoided goods on freight which might compete with their own. If we may judge from their practice, most of the great merchants must have agreed with John Reynell when he said 'the West India trade in a generall way is grown much worse than it was, and nowadays there's seldom any thing to be gott by shipping goods there on

[1] *Letter-Book of John Watts* (*N[ew] Y[ork] H[istorical] S[ociety] Collections*, lxi), p. 17; John Reynell to Henry Sherburne, 23 January 1740/1, Reynell Letter-Book B, p. 121, H.S.P.

[2] William Lux wrote to his brother, 1 February 1764, that he had been offered a freight to Barbados, but 'as I had about 300 Bbs flour ready and a prospect of a great crop at Barbados I thought it best not to take it' (Letter-Book of William Lux, N.Y.H.S.). John Reynell's correspondents at Antigua advised him in October 1751 that many people would overrate the effects of the recent hurricane at the Leeward Islands and ship goods thither, so that it would be to his interest to accept a freight rather than send his vessel there on his own account (Birkett and Booth to J. Reynell, 21 October 1751, Reynell Papers, Box vi, H.S.P.) See also Jonathan Dickinson to John Lewis, n.d. and 7 December 1718, Letter-Book of Jonathan Dickinson, pp. 182, 231, L.C.P.

[3] Very often an owner who had taken goods on freight for the West Indies would instruct his captain to invest the freight-money, which would be receivable there, in West India produce and bring home, besides, any goods he could obtain on freight.

[4] This is why Messrs. Greg and Cunningham asked their agents in Barbados to try to arrange that any goods taken on freight in the return voyage should be consigned to themselves 'as by that means the price won't be pulled down' (Greg and Cunningham to Walker and Woodbridge, Barbados, 12 July 1756, Letter-Book of Greg and Cunningham, pp. 81–2, N.Y.H.S.)

freight, if there's any thing to be gott it must be by owners of vessells.'[1]

II. THE SHIPS

These vessels were owned sometimes by a single merchant or firm, sometimes by a partnership. Shares of a quarter, an eighth, or even a sixteenth were not unknown: Timothy Orne of Salem took very small shares in a number of vessels—a habit which was probably characteristic of the Salem fishing industry.[2] Some ship-owning partnerships were formed, as I have already said, between West Indians and North Americans. These had the advantage of interesting both partners permanently in the despatch of the vessel, but they tended to restrict her to the trade of a particular island. Such a restriction, common enough on the routes between British ports and the West Indies, had less to recommend it when there was no question of cultivating the planters' goodwill for the sake of a freight of sugar; and, although several North Americans spoke of 'fixing' a vessel in the trade, for example, between Philadelphia and Jamaica,[3] when it came to the point they often wished to depart from this arrangement, and valued the freedom to do so, which a partner in the islands might inhibit.

Much was written about the kinds and, still more, the size of the vessels in this trade; but most of it was inconclusive, like the other generalizations which merchants uttered under the influence of ignorant optimism or disappointment. Many of the markets in the islands were so small that a large vessel could easily glut them by herself, even without any competitors.[4] (This consideration helps, no doubt, to account for the great variety of goods carried in the average cargo.) On the other hand, some merchants described a small vessel as a 'pick-

---

[1] J. Reynell to M. L. Dicker, 28 June 1738, Reynell Letter-Book B, p. 65, H.S.P.

[2] See his papers in the Essex Institute, Salem, Mass. His smallest share was one-sixteenth, his largest seven-eighths.

[3] For example, Isaac Norris in 1701 (Norris to Richard Sleigh, 11 September 1701, Norris Letter-Book, i, 345, H.S.P.).

[4] 'People rather ship in a small vessell than in a large one because a large one is apt to glutt a market' (John Reynell to Richard Deeble, 29 May 1734, Reynell Letter-Book A, p. 80, H.S.P.). This actually happened to the Brig *Caesar* at Basseterre, Guadeloupe, in 1765 (Josiah Orne to owners of Brig *Caesar*, 5 December 1765, Timothy Orne MSS., xii, 64, Essex Institute).

pocket'—she paid the same port dues as a larger one, and was navigated with only one or two fewer hands.[1] In particular, a vessel which might be intended to pick up a freight from the islands to Great Britain must be big enough to carry sugar hogsheads—she should not be too sharp, and she should carry two decks.[2] So far as one can state averages, one may say that such a vessel might average 120 to 140 tons, whereas one which was likely to be confined to American waters might measure 50 to 80 tons. The requirements of the trade were not specialized. Not only might the same crews and vessels which had brought the rum and molasses be employed during the winter in peddling it to Virginia or Maryland, but we catch sight of an occasional whaler in the West India trade.[3] On the other hand, it was held to be a mistake to use an ocean-going vessel as a sugar-droger—that is, for the coastwise trade of the island; she would be too sharp, and a few months of beating up against a trade-wind with a cargo of rum on her deck would strain her beyond repair.[4]

It is difficult to estimate the number of voyages which such a vessel would make annually, supposing her to go to and fro between the continent and the islands. Schemes were sometimes laid for as many as four in a year;[5] but I doubt if these can have been realized often. It is hard to be sure of this, for few vessels did, in practice, ply straight to and fro in this way. But I think that six voyages in two years—the greatest number I can prove—was quite a good performance.[6] The hitch commonly resulted, not from the vessels' own limitations, but (as I shall hope to show later) from the difficulty of selling the cargo and obtaining returns. But there were also some natural hindrances to the *perpetuum mobile* which every ship-owner

[1] J. Reynell to M. L. Dicker, 3 October 1733, Reynell Papers, Box i, H.S.P.

[2] Jonathan Dickinson to Jonathan Gale, 30 April 1715, Letter-Book of Jonathan Dickinson, p. 21, L.C.P.; James Hudson to William Rathbone, 30 July 1757, Hudson Collection, Account-Book 1756–1788, N.Y.P.L.

[3] Silvanus Hussey to Nicholas Brown and Co., 2 November 1763, Brown MSS., J.C.B.L.

[4] Jonathan Dickinson to (?) Isaac Gale, 9 December 1717, Letter-Book of Jonathan Dickinson, p. 170, L.C.P.

[5] Henry Bonnin to John Reynell, 16 May 1733, Reynell Papers, Box i, H.S.P.

[6] John Reynell claimed this for a vessel he owned to M. L. Dicker, 15 September 1735 (Reynell Papers, Box i, H.S.P.).

C

desired. Not every ship-owner, and certainly not every
insurer, liked to have a vessel among the islands in the hurricane months, August to October; and the ice closed most of
the northern rivers from the beginning of January to early
March. These two things created a certain rhythm in the year:
everybody who could, got his vessel away from the coast before
the ice (often glutting the island markets in consequence), and
hoped to get her back in April with the first rum or molasses
of the crop; after this, there should be time for one more
voyage out and home (but not two, unless one cared to risk the
hurricanes), before the ice came down again.[1] But this picture
is simplified: it makes no allowance for the numerous coasting
voyages, with West India goods, from Boston to Newfoundland
in the summer-time or from Rhode Island or Philadelphia to
the tobacco colonies in the winter—one enterprising man even
transferred his winter headquarters from Philadelphia to ice-
free Charleston,[2] and many others made three-cornered
voyages between a northern continental port, a southern continental port, and the islands.

The crews were small: twelve or even ten would be a large
crew for a vessel of under 100 tons, unless she were a privateer
in war-time.[3] Not very much is known of their provenance;
but it is doubtful how far sailors were a specialized and permanent class before the Revolution. There may have been a
small nucleus of regular sailors: a Massachusetts firm with
interests in whaling or fishing once explained that they were

[1] The following figures for the arrivals and departures of vessels in the West
India trade at Boston, 1752, are instructive:

	Jan.	*Feb.*	*March*	*April*	*May*	*June*
Departures	21	12	9	8	13	10
Arrivals	7	2	8	14	15	14
	July	*Aug.*	*Sept.*	*Oct.*	*Nov.*	*Dec.*
Departures	11	6	6	5	8	13
Arrivals	12	9	4	5	3	6

(Mass. H.S., MSS., 91 L., p. 44)

The arrivals in this table do not balance the departures: for an explanation of this
see page 48.

[2] Robert Ellis, whose letter-book is preserved in the Historical Society of Pennsylvania.

[3] The Browns' Sloop *George* usually sailed with a crew of nine or ten (including
one or two coopers) besides the master; their Brigantine *Sally* with eight or nine
(likewise including coopers), their Brigantine *Providence* with eleven, their Sloop
Four Brothers, it seems, with only four or five (Brown MSS., J.C.B.L.).

sending a vessel on a winter voyage to Virginia because they could not hope to find three crews in the summer if they did not keep one together in the winter.[1] But the whaling and fishing were rather a specialized business; and the average North American sailor, used to short voyages of four or five months, was much less completely divorced from the land than the English seaman. Probably this fact explains why the Americans were so much less ready than the Englishmen to acquiesce in the press-gang. Nobody liked the press-gang, of course; but impressment only meant, for many English sailors, the substitution of one long voyage for another. The Americans, a century before the incident of the *Chesapeake* and the *Leopard* made impressment an international issue, would do anything to avoid the proximity of the Royal Navy. It was seriously suggested by Governors of Jamaica (who, indeed, had an axe of their own to sharpen against the naval commanders) that fear of impressment created a shortage of provisions by scaring the North Americans away from the island; and the same argument was used against any Admiral who was ready to send his prisoners of war to Europe in war-time, at the risk of the enemy following his example.[2] These arguments may have been strained; for, though such statistics as we have seem to show that the West India trade (where the press-gangs were to be encountered) was slightly more depressed in war-time than some other branches of North American commerce, the difference is not marked enough to be conclusive.[3]

[1] Samuel Lee to Timothy Orne, 29 November 1758, Timothy Orne MSS., iii, 143, Essex Institute.

[2] *Calendar of State Papers, America and West Indies, 1696–7*, nos. 97, 639; *1700*, nos. 15, 66. See also my articles on 'The Manning of the Navy in the West Indies, 1702–1763', in *Trans. Royal Hist. Soc.*, 4th Series, xx, 31–60, and on 'Prisoners of War in the West Indies', *Journal of the Barbados Museum and Historical Society*, vol. v.

[3] The New York statistics (*Calendar of State Papers, America and West Indies, 1716–1717*, no. 470) show that ships trading to Europe averaged 15.8 annually in the war years 1705–11, 22.6 in the peace years 1712–16; ships trading to the West Indies, 62 and 97.6 respectively; ships trading to the other continental colonies (the trade freest from press-gangs and other war risks) 52.8 and 58 respectively. The shipping returns of Kingston, Jamaica (Public Record Office, C.O. 142/15) show that in 1744 arrivals from the northern colonies were 149 out of 321; in 1745, 103 out of 276; in 1746, 104 out of 250; in the peaceful year Michaelmas 1751 to Michaelmas 1752, 164 out of 369.

The sailors' duties included such odds and ends as bundling shingles for the market,[1] fetching molasses on rafts up and down the rivers of Surinam,[2] and, perhaps, collecting barrow-loads of salt at Salt Tortuga (though some owners ordered their captains to take on extra hands for this duty at Barbados.)[3] For setting up the hogsheads to carry molasses (which the planters sold from the cistern) many vessels carried their own coopers; if a cooper died or fell ill, or none was sent, the captain might find himself completely paralysed, for, though most plantations had negro coopers of their own, these might all be preoccupied in crop-time.[4]

The payment of sailors' wages created a peculiar difficulty in a country where cash was always scarce. (Jonathan Dickinson once reported that molasses was selling unusually low in Philadelphia in order to raise money for this purpose.)[5] The owners resorted to some curious expedients in order to overcome this difficulty. Sailors were sometimes paid in kind: an agreement concerning an early voyage to the wine islands provides for part payment in fish and in West India produce.[6] But the commonest expedient was that of supplementing the wage by the 'privilege' of loading so many barrels or hogsheads on the outward and homeward voyage on the sailors' own account. This was a way of forcing the crew to participate in the risks of the voyage, but it had its dangers, for if a lawful trader met an enemy privateer in war-time or an unlawful trader met a British man-of-war, the captor might bribe the master or crew into disclosing something to the owners' dis-

---

[1] Log-book of the Sloop *Elizabeth*, M. 656—1769 E, Essex Institute.

[2] Orders to Captain Simon Smith, 9 December 1768, Brown MSS., papers of Brigantine *Sally*, J.C.B.L.

[3] Joseph and William Atkins and Jonathan Barnard's instructions to Captain James Hudson, 16 January 1746/7: to make the best of his way from Barbados to Salt Tortuga 'having bags and barrows and your men upon high wages for the purpose of going to that island to get a load salt'. (Hudson-Rogers Papers, Box i, N.Y.P.L.)

[4] Captain Hawkins of the Browns' Sloop *Four Brothers* found himself in this condition at Surinam, December 1766. (Hawkins to Nicholas Brown and Co., 24 December 1766, Brown MSS., J.C.B.L.)

[5] Jonathan Dickinson to Lewis Galdy, 27 April 1717, Letter-Book of Jonathan Dickinson, p. 131, L.C.P.; to Jonathan Gale, 11 June 1718, *ibid.*, p. 200.

[6] *Essex County, Records and Files of the Quarterly Court* (Salem, 1911), ii, 392 (wage agreement of the Ship *Ann*).

advantage by promising to restore their private adventures.[1]
Also the sailors might get the ship into trouble by selling their
privilege cargoes in contravention of some customs regulation,
French or British[2]—to say nothing of the ever-present danger
that their competition in the market would pull down the
price of the main cargo.[3] On the other hand, it sometimes
enabled the owners to apply a sanction—as when the Browns
decreed that if any of their sailors in the river of Surinam
accepted bad molasses on one of the rafting trips, he should be
made to take it as part of his privilege.[4] At any rate, the practice was nearly universal; and it looks as though the privilege
was considered more important than the money wage, for the
grades on board ship were differentiated much more sharply
by the former than by the latter; an officer's wage was little
larger than a common seaman's, his privilege much larger.[5]
This was particularly noticeable in the relation of the cooper
and the master of the vessel: the cooper's money wage was

[1] This offer was made in vain to Captain James Duncan of Rhode Island in
1767 (*Commerce of Rhode Island*, ed. W. C. Ford, *Mass. H.S. Collections*, 7th series,
ix, 86).

[2] The owners of the Schooner *Volant* instructed the master on 29 December 1741,
in case he should go to the French islands 'to give strict orders amongst your men
not to sell the least trifle unto them on any terms least they should make your
vessel liable to a seizure' (Derby Family MSS., x, 2, Essex Institute).

[3] Captain Simon Gross of the *Charming Lydia* promised (28 November 1742) to
offer his private venture to the consignee of the cargo 'pour ne pas faire tort a la
ditte cargaison' (Hancock MSS., Harvard University, Graduate School of
Business Administration). The sailors usually disposed of their privilege cargoes
freely, at any rate on the homeward voyage, for Joshua Hempstead, of New
London, sometimes bought rum and molasses of them (see his *Diary*, *New London
Hist. Soc. Collections*, vol. i *passim*.). On the other hand, Timothy Orne instructed
the master of a vessel carrying rum and molasses from Salem to Maryland not to
let his men 'retail out their rum and molasses' (Timothy Orne MSS., vol. vi,
Essex Institute).

[4] Orders to Captain Simon Smith, 9 December 1768, Brown MSS., papers of
Brigantine *Sally*, J.C.B.L.

[5] To take some examples from the Brown MSS.: on the Sloop *George*, in 1763, the
master had £35 (Old Tenor currency) per month and 10 hogsheads privilege, the
sailors ranged from £60 and 8 barrels to £40 and 3 barrels; on the Sloop *Four
Brothers*, 1766, the master had £35 per month and 8 hogsheads, two of the sailors
had £50 and no privilege; on the Brigantine *Sally*, 1767, the master had £60 and
7 hogsheads, the sailors varied from £50 and 2 barrels to £24 and no privilege.
One thing about these portledge bills shows the conservatism of the Rhode Island
sailor: for some years after the Browns had begun to reckon their cargoes in the
newer currency known as Lawful Money they continued to reckon the wages in
Old Tenor.

often greater than the master's (perhaps because it represented what he could have earned ashore) but his privilege was much less, indeed he sometimes had none at all.[1]

One might wonder where the crews of these vessels found the money for these private ventures, which formed so important a part of their income. Often, no doubt, the captain, with the owner's consent, would advance money or molasses to them: it is certain, for example, that this was done on some of the Browns' vessels. Other sailors borrowed the money on a kind of bottomry from small capitalists.[2] Bottomry bonds had been a quite common form of maritime investment in the seventeenth century, and the early records of this trade show some examples of it.[3] But the practice seems to have lost its importance in the eighteenth century, and the only large collection of anything resembling bottomry contracts that I have found is among the papers of that curiously old-fashioned business man Timothy Orne of Salem. Nearly all these bonds represent loans made to seamen, doubtless for the purpose of financing the exploitation of their 'privileges' on West India voyages. For example, in November 1759, Timothy Orne lends Samuel Carlton, junior, of Salem, mariner, £26 13s. 4d. Lawful Money on the bottom of the Schooner *Dolphin* on a voyage to the Virgin or Leeward Islands and back, and to go coasting and freighting between Guadeloupe and Grande Terre for any time between the date of the contract and the next hurricane season. If the schooner is sold, the money to be on the bottom of any vessel on which her effects are shipped to Salem. If she goes to the Leeward or Virgin Islands and returns without going to Guadeloupe, the money to be repaid on return with 35 per cent advance. If she goes to Guadeloupe or Grande Terre but does not go freighting, with 40 per cent;

---

[1] On the voyages of the *George* and the *Sally* referred to in the preceding note, the respective coopers got £80 per month with 4 hogsheads, 2 barrels privilege, and £55 per month with 7 barrels privilege. The *Four Brothers*, for some reason, carried no cooper. Timothy Orne's coopers usually had the same wages as the mates.

[2] Strictly, bottomry was a contract by which the owner or master of the ship pledged her as security for a loan to be repaid with interest at the end of the voyage. In this trade the sailors, though holding no interest in the ship, could borrow money on similar terms, giving bond for repayment.

[3] e.g. in *Aspinwall Notarial Records*, pp. 11, 258; *Suffolk Deeds*, i, 255.

if she goes freighting, with 50 per cent; and if at any point in her voyage she takes a load of salt, 2 per cent extra to be paid. Carlton gives bond in £60 Lawful Money for the execution of this contract. The whole thing reads rather like an insurance policy, but the rates of 'advance' are much higher than the insurance premiums.[1]

Insurance itself is the last form of maritime investment which ought to be mentioned here. Some merchants in North America insured their ventures in London, but the London underwriters disliked policies for vessels whose condition they could not judge because they had never seen them, on cross voyages whose risks they could not estimate, stuffed with all sorts of contingent additions or returns of premiums according as the vessel might touch at this island or not touch at that. They would protect themselves by charging higher premiums than an American underwriter, and they might refuse to touch the policy at all.[2] Most of this business was therefore done by Americans. Not every seaport on the continent had its own insurance office: for example, Portsmouth, New Hampshire, had not, and the merchants had to apply to the Philadelphia insurers.[3] But the West India traders of any port, however small, might enter into mutual insurance contracts like that by which William Lynde and Timothy Orne of Salem undertook to insure each other's vessels on their voyages to the West Indies for the sum of £200 each way.[4] Even at Philadelphia, probably the chief centre for insurance on the continent, the underwriting had some aspects of a mutual insurance scheme: for of the 23 underwriters whose names are recorded as insuring the West India voyages of John Reynell, mostly for very small

[1] This contract is in vol. iii of the Timothy Orne MSS., Essex Institute. There are many other such in the same collection. Timothy Orne was not quite the only person to lend money in this way: Joshua Hempstead of New London records in his *Diary* (p. 97) that he delivered a ship's captain £5 in silver Barbados money to buy rum in Barbados. This was very likely a bottomry loan.

[2] Lane and Caswall, London, to Timothy Orne, 7 August 1745, Timothy Orne MSS., xi, 10, Essex Institute; Daniel Flexney, London, to John Reynell, 9 September 1746, Reynell Papers, Box iii, H.S.P.

[3] John Sherburne and John Moffatt, merchants of Portsmouth, both wrote often for insurance to John Reynell of Philadelphia.

[4] Timothy Orne MSS., i, 33, Essex Institute. Obadiah and Elisha Brown of Providence, Rhode Island, made a similar arrangement in 1746 (Journal of Obadiah Brown, 1746–51, R[hode] I[sland] H[istorical] S[ociety]).

sums,[1] at least five are known to me as having been West India merchants themselves, and these include three whose names appear upon the policies most frequently.[2]

III. THE PORTS

The active merchant class, whose business I have been describing, was located at a dozen or so of seaports up and down the coast, of which Boston, Philadelphia, New York and Newport were easily the most important by 1740—the ascent of Providence and, later, Baltimore only became visible shortly before the Revolution, and neither Charleston nor even Salem quite rivalled the four big ports in this trade. Of these, Boston was the oldest and for a long time the greatest: it was described in 1675 as 'a magazine both of all American and Europian commodityes for the furnishing and supplying of the seaverall countreys',[3] and Edmund Randolph, who doubtless exaggerated the illicit prosperity which he envied and wished to destroy, described the merchants of New England as trading generally with most parts of Europe, exporting colonial produce and bringing back European goods which they distributed among the West Indies.[4] The Bostonians themselves preserved into the eighteenth century a tradition of this pre-eminence; but in fact they began to lose it after the Peace of Utrecht, if not before.

The relative decline of Boston resulted, in part, from natural causes—above all, from the extension of settlement eastwards and, still more, southwards. This extension required, in the first place, the felling of trees along thousands of miles of sea-

---

[1] The insured preferred a number of small subscriptions to a few great ones, as it spread the risk of encountering sharp practice (Nicholas Brown and Co. to David Van Horn, New York, 11 February 1766, Brown MSS., J.C.B.L.).

[2] Reynell Papers, Box xiii, H.S.P.

[3] 'A narrative of the settlement of the corporaĉon of the Massachusetts Bay . . . received from Mr. Mason 1st Xber 1675', Public Record Office, C.O. 1/35, no. 50.

[4] C.O. 1/37, no. 70. The eminence of Boston about 1700 can be judged by some trade statistics of New York, 1 January 1700–31 December 1701 and 1 January–31 July 1703 (those of 1702 are, for some reason, missing). Of 112,836 gallons of rum imported, 56,115 gallons came from Barbados, 19,689 gallons from Boston, and only 803 from all other continental ports together. (New York City, Hall of Records, Old Conveyances, Lib. 30.)

coast and river-bank, which released staves and other lumber
from new areas for the West Indies. The deforestation was
followed by the cultivation of new staples, or of the old staples
over again, and this produce too was ready to be carried to the
islands from ports further and further removed from Boston:
Virginia and Carolina pork might not be so good as Burlington
pork, nor Baltimore flour so good as New York flour; but they
were good enough for the West India market. The geographical
results of this dispersion can be seen if we examine the exports from North America to the West Indies in 1771 in
order to discover the ports from which the largest quantities of
each article went. I give, for each principal article, the two
ports with the greatest exports, with their figures:

Candles, spermaceti, lb.	Rhode Island (251,180), Boston (55,710)
Candles, tallow, lb.	New York (64,500), Philadelphia (17,400)
Corn, bushels	James River (Va.) (lower parts) (228,376), New York (63,319)
Lard, lb.	New York (44,140), Rhode Island (37,640)
Leather, lb.	Charleston (S.C.) (13,720), Philadelphia (4,024)
Onions, ropes	New London (105,394), Rhode Island (83,248)
Bricks	Piscataqua (496,500), Boston (341,800)
Oak boards, feet	Philadelphia (88,600), New London (65,510)
Pine boards, feet	Piscataqua (13,197,360), Falmouth (4,527,250)
Shook hogsheads[1]	Salem and Marblehead (15,513), Boston (12,539)
Shingles	Piscataqua (6,092,000), James River (lower parts) (5,816,435)
Hoops	Rhode Island (1,309,750), Boston (513,580)
Staves	Philadelphia (2,806,068), James River (lower parts) (1,944,230)
Rice, barrels	Charleston (27,300), Savannah (1,677)

[1] 'Shook hogsheads' or 'shaken hogsheads' was a term applied to the staves and
heading in bundles before they were made into hogsheads.

Loaf sugar, lb.	New York (4,362), Philadelphia (3,150)
Cattle	New London (1,456), New Haven (1,373)
Horses	New London (3,162), New Haven (1,305)
Hogs and sheep	New London (4,182), Rhode Island (2,966)
Poultry, dozen	Rhode Island (1,052), New London (1,019)
Bread and flour, tons	Philadelphia (12,253), New York (3,250)
Beef and pork, barrels	James River (lower parts) (4,198) Philadelphia (3,360)
Butter, lb.	New York (35,100), Charleston (24,260)
Cheese, lb.	Rhode Island (71,678), New London (31,986)
Dried fish, quintals	Salem and Marblehead (87,889), Boston (57,492)
Pickled fish, barrels	Rhode Island (14,902), Boston (8,386)
Pease and beans, bushels	James River (lower parts) (9,894), Charleston (6,305)

Boston does not appear once at the head of these tables, and
seldom even occupies the second place except in articles which
have been processed, however slightly. When we look, however, at the movement of West India produce and of manufactures derived from it, we see her partly restored to her
original importance. Her total imports of molasses from the
West Indies amounted in this year to 1,096,496 gallons—she
was followed by Salem with 637,854 gallons and by Rhode
Island with 502,380 gallons, then by New York, Philadelphia
and Piscataqua, each of which imported between 400,000 and
500,000 gallons. In 1769, her surplus of molasses exported
coastwise over molasses imported coastwise was 191,732 gallons.
Rhode Island had an even larger surplus of 228,332 gallons;
New London had a surplus of 117,866 gallons—mostly peddled
out in Long Island, no doubt—and Salem a surplus of 78,933
gallons—but no other port had a significant surplus at all. It
is clear, then, that the New England ports retained the lead in
the distribution of West India produce, and this fact creates a

reasonable suspicion that much of the lumber and provisions was carried from other parts of the continent to the islands in the ships of New Englanders and on their account. But Boston's performance in the article of rum is even more striking. The New England ports did not import much West India rum—in 1769 Boston took only 71,937 gallons, Rhode Island 155,410 gallons (of which two-thirds was re-exported), New London 209,413 gallons (of which nearly half was re-exported) and Salem a mere 78,266 gallons: these figures are nothing to those of Philadelphia, which imported 734,242 gallons from the islands as well as 12,860 gallons in the coastwise trade, and only passed on, of this total, 89,409 gallons; or of New York, which imported 211,461 gallons from the islands and 208,764 gallons coastwise, and only re-exported 18,267 gallons. But although Boston did not make a living by distributing West India rum among the centres of consumption to the south-wards (the frontiersmen to the east of her were almost too frugal to drink it at all), she distilled her vast imports of molasses into the cheaper New England rum: she exported 535,538 gallons more of this article than she imported. The corresponding figures for Rhode Island were 238,302 gallons and for Salem 117,901. New London imported twice as much New England rum as she exported (both figures were small): she might distribute West India rum to the Long Islanders, but she did not distil for them. New York's exports of North American rum exceeded her imports by 119,114 gallons, but no port further south had a surplus at all—not even Philadelphia. South of the Mason-Dixon line we are in the land of the heavy drinkers, who import large quantities both of West Indian and American rum, and hardly re-export a drop of either.[1]

The dispersion of trade, especially of the export trade, which these figures reveal was not the result of natural causes alone; it was artificially speeded by provincial regulations. Connecticut did not wish to remain forever a mere agricultural hinterland of Boston, nor Maryland of Philadelphia. The authorities of Connecticut reported in 1680 that the colony was still a dependency of Boston: 'In our colony there are about 20 petty

[1] The figures I have been discussing come from the statistical abstracts in the Massachusetts Historical Society's papers.

merchants. Som trade only to Boston, som to Boston and the Indies, others to Boston and New York, others to Boston, the Indies and Newfoundland', and the miserable catalogue of shipping, amounting in all to 1,050 tons, confirms the justice of this description.[1] But their successors resolved to remedy this state of affairs: from 1708 the General Assembly started to discriminate, in its tax laws, in favour of wines and rum 'imported directly from the place of their making or growth, and in vessels part owned by one or more inhabitants of this colony'.[2] The Connecticut legislators likewise tried to reserve the export trade in lumber for their own merchants: an 'Act for the Preservation of Timber' in 1714 imposed a tax on barrel staves shipped from the ports of Connecticut to any other colony between New Hampshire and New Jersey.[3] One might have thought that Massachusetts could afford to put up with this kind of thing without retaliating: but its General Court likewise imposed, in 1746, double duties on goods not coming from the ports of their growth, and not belonging to inhabitants of the colony.[4] Maryland and Pennsylvania bickered at each other in the same way, from as early as 1698: Maryland penalized the importation of rum from Pennsylvania, especially by land, and sometimes laid a tax upon Maryland produce exported by non-residents.[5] Pennsylvania too had her discriminatory duties.

This legislation was not always effective: it is a great mistake to suppose that the trade laws of the imperial parliament were the only ones to be evaded by smugglers.[6] So far as it was obeyed, it seems to have injured not only the merchants of the rival continental ports, but also such West Indians as might be

---

[1] *Connecticut Public Records*, iii, 297.

[2] *Ibid.*, v, 84; vi, 36, 282; vii, 565; ix, 283. The discrimination originally took the form of a total exemption from the duty, later of admission at a lower rate.

[3] *Ibid.*, v, 434; a similar Act was passed again in 1747 (*ibid.*, ix, 286).

[4] C.O. 5/882.

[5] *Archives of Maryland* (ed. Maryland Hist. Soc.), xxii, 29; xxvi, 276, 281, 349; xxxix, 74–80; see also Governor Sharpe's letters, *ibid.*, iii, 72, 99. A full account of this sort of legislation is given by A. A. Giesecke, *American Commercial Legislation before 1789* (New York, 1910).

[6] There exists in the Brown MSS. (J.C.B.L.) a letter of 1 February 1763 from Carter Braxton of Virginia, explaining how to elude by a false clearance a discriminatory law of this sort.

inclined to ship produce to the continent on their own account. ⟩
Perhaps it was not always meant to do so: only in the preamble
of the Massachusetts Act of 1738 do we find any evidence o
such an intention.[1] But it might do so unintentionally. Not
everybody thought this fair.[2] The West Indian colonies may
have taxed transient traders and so incidentally discriminated
in favour of their own resident merchants;[3] but they did not
discourage inhabitants of other parts of the empire from taking
an active part in the trade. But, fair or not, the northern
colonies discriminated in favour of their own against West
Indian enterprise; and this may be one of the reasons why there
was, as I have argued already, so little West Indian enterprise
in this trade.

The figures which I have been discussing show that the one
branch of the West India trade where Boston still retained a
lead, even over Rhode Island, on the eve of the Revolution,
was the distilling of West India molasses into rum.

The North American distilleries did not develop without a
struggle: they had to contend with adverse prejudices and even
laws, especially in New England. The motives of this legislation were three. The oldest and strongest was the desire to
protect the Red Indians from the temptation to 'that greate

[1] 'And whereas many strangers and foreigners have of late years reaped great
gain and profit by bringing into this province considerable quantities of foreign
molasses and rum on their own accounts whereby much of the trade that was
formerly carried on with considerable profit by the inhabitants of this province
although with the paying very high charges for permission, etc., in their islands is
in a great measure, if not wholly, prevented.' The Act goes on to impose an additional duty upon molasses imported by foreigners. (C.O. 5/882.) The words 'in
their islands' seem to show that this Act was meant primarily to discriminate
against West Indians—probably French West Indians.

[2] Jonathan Dickinson of Philadelphia pointed out (to Isaac Gale, 10 May 1721)
that 'All the rum from our own Plant^a pay a duty of 2d p gall^o here that is on acct of
any person not resident in this province. Our traders bring in Dutch rum and pay
not one doit.' (Letter-Book of Jonathan Dickinson, p. 379, L.C.P.) This expres-
sion is interesting, since Dickinson had interests both in Jamaica and in Pennsylvania, and must have thought of himself both as a Jamaican and as a Penn-
sylvanian. He evidently had no sympathy with the West Indian agitation for
prohibiting trade between the northern colonies and the foreign sugar colonies
(see the earlier part of the letter quoted), but he thought the discriminatory
taxation of Pennsylvania unfair to the British West Indies.

[3] So did some of the northern colonies (e.g. Rhode Island, by Acts of 1739 and
1750). I shall deal later (pp. 69–70) with the taxation of transient traders in the
West Indies.

& crying sinn of drunkenes . . . to the great dishonor of God
& hazard of the lives & peace boath of the English & Indyans'.[1]
The laws for this purpose were never completely enforced, and
perhaps, as the Indians were gradually removed from the main
centres of population, few people took much interest in the
matter; it was left to the colonial Governors appointed by the
Crown to feel the sting of the reproach 'even from the *Popish*
missionaries among the *Indians*, that while they are teaching
those poor people vertue and religion, we are destroying their
souls and bodies with a *plague of rum*, for so they stile it'. A
second motive was the prejudice against rum itself: the seven-
teenth-century colonists who were used to beer[2] and had not
yet experienced the horrors of gin, might well feel an aversion
to a drink which even the West Indians themselves called 'kill
devil'. The General Court of Connecticut forbade its importation altogether in 1654, though, four years later, they
confined the penalties to consumption within the colony,
allowing their subjects to profit from the sins and diseases of
others by re-exporting the accursed thing.[3] Later in the history of the colony these prohibitions were replaced by milder
and more profitable import duties: that of 1720 was almost
prohibitive at £15 the hogshead, as one might expect from the
preamble which complained that 'many mischiefs are grown
upon too many of the inhabitants of this government, even to
the threatning them in many, if not all, their interests, by means
of the great quantities of rhum that are imported into this
colony and here consumed'. But a new law, only the very next
year, began the decline of morality into fiscality and even pro-
tectionism by substituting a duty of 4d. per gallon, or even 3d.

---

[1] Order of General Court, (?) 6 April 1654, *Connecticut Public Records*, i, 263. This
order was made without reference to rum, but rum was mentioned in some of the
later laws, and in the correspondence between the Governors of Massachusetts and
the General Court, May–June 1718, July 1720, December 1730 (*Journals of the
House of Representatives of Massachusetts* (Mass. H.S. edition), ii, 5, 46, 48, 55–6, 255;
ix, 351, 383).

[2] The people of Massachusetts also complained that the brewers 'take liberty
to make & sell drinck brued of or mixed with molasses, course sugars or other
materialls, to the damage, just offence, & prejudice of sundry persons', instead of
putting the proper quantity of malt into the beer. (*Records of the Colony of the
Massachusetts Bay in New England*, ed. Shurtleff, iv, part ii, 344.)

[3] *Connecticut Public Records*, ii, 255, 322.

if the rum were imported directly from the West Indies in a
Connecticut vessel.[1] The authorities of the colony showed their
good faith for a short time by prohibiting the distilling of
molasses 'for that by said practice molasses is made scarce and
dear, and the spirits drawn off there from are usually very unwholesome, and of little value';[2] the same motive had already,
nine years earlier, inspired a bill in Massachusetts 'to prevent
scarcity of molasses by its being distilled into rum'.[3] The
Massachusetts bill seems to have come to nothing, and even the
Connecticut law lasted no longer than five months, for it was
conditional on the virtue of others: it had to be repealed, on the
ground that 'the said neighbouring governments still allowing
the distilling of molasses, while prohibited here in this colony,
draws, or is like to draw, the whole trade of molasses from the
West Indies'.[4]

These discouragements were not nearly whole-hearted
enough to stop the drinking and distilling of rum. It began on
a large scale in Boston, somewhere about 1700; its progress
there can be partly traced by the grants of licences to distillers.
In considering applications, the Selectmen appear to have had
in mind, above all, the location of the still-houses, whose nasty
smells and refuse made them a nuisance and a danger to
health.[5] They were also concerned to take sureties against
liability to support immigrant distillers who might fall into
indigence,[6] and once, at least, warned such a person to depart,
'as more of that imploym^t is not needfull in this town'.[7] These
precautions did not prevent occasional unemployment in the
Boston distilleries, for the town meeting of 27 May 1752 complained that 'six still houses are wholly unoccupied and there
is not one in the town, fully and steadily employed and most of
them are not half improved'.[7] The size of the industry is hard

---

[1] *Ibid.*, vi, 223, 282.　　　　　　　　[2] *Ibid.*, vii, 110.

[3] *Journals of the House of Representatives of Massachusetts*, ii, 46. The Selectmen of
Boston had tried even earlier, in 1710, to promote such a bill (Boston Record
Commissioners, *Boston Town Records, 1701–1715*, p. 108).

[4] *Connecticut Public Records*, vii, 138.

[5] Meeting of Selectmen, 6 June 1692, Boston Records Commissioners, *Boston
Town Records, 1660–1701*, p. 215.

[6] Meeting of 25 January 1714/15, *ibid.*, p. 221.

[7] Meeting of 3 May 1715, *ibid.*, p. 227.

[8] *Boston Town Records, 1742–1747*, p. 221.

to judge: statistics of exports by sea would not give its full measure. A Boston merchant, calculating the damage likely to result from the Boston Port Act of 1774, appears to say that the turn-over (he surely cannot mean the profit) would amount to £6,000 Lawful Money per week.[1] Such calculations are guesses: perhaps it is more significant that in 1780 there were at least 18 distillers in Boston, excluding distillery employees, and that the aggregate rental of their premises was £4,295. The number is almost certainly an under-estimate, for occupations are only given in 9½ out of the town's 12 wards. But it is clear that the distillers' premises were larger and more expensive than almost any others, and theirs seems to have been one of the principal industries of the town.[2]

Even in the distillery Boston began, soon after 1700, to feel the draught of competition. In the town's requests to the General Court for relief from taxation (a most unreliable source of information, to be sure) the decline of the distillery and its dispersion into the other towns of Massachusetts, or even into other colonies altogether, is frequently lamented. Thus on 28 May 1746 the town complains that its distilleries are only working half time from scarcity of molasses, that what molasses they have is mostly imported by merchants of Salem and other outports of the province whose navigation is cheaper, and that the business of distilling is itself carried on at Charlestown, Watertown, Medford and Nantucket. In May 1752 'six still houses are wholly unoccupied and there is not one in the town, fully and steadily employed, and most of them are not half improved, owing not only to the great increase of still-houses at Rhode Island, and to great numbers very lately erected at New York and Philadelphia, but also too many set up in this province'. They claimed, next year, in a historical retrospect, that the town had 'about forty years since, begun a considerable branch of business by distilling molasses or treacle as it is called at home, and refining sugar; these manufactures for near twenty years were wholly confined to the town of

[1] John Andrews to W. Barrell, 20 August 1774, printed in *Proceedings of the Massachusetts Historical Society*, 1st series, viii, 344.

[2] Assessors' Books of the Town of Boston, 1780, *Publications of the Bostonian Society*, ix, 15–59.

Boston, and there was scarcely a still house or sugar house anywhere else, in this or any of the neighbouring governments'.[1] This was an exaggeration; but undoubtedly the Boston distillers and sugar-refiners had once had things their own way for a short time, and did so no longer. The *American Weekly Mercury* of Philadelphia, which had only found it worth while in April 1739 to distinguish New England from West India rum in its prices current, was now, by the date of the last of these petitions, quoting the prices of Pennsylvania rum as well; it had sometimes distinguished Boston from London refined sugar in the 1720's, but from February 1738–9 it regularly printed the prices of Philadelphia loaf sugar, and Boston sugar was mentioned no more. This too was a natural and inevitable thing: when all ports were equally open to West India produce, it was too much to expect the simpler processing industries to remain concentrated in one of them for ever.

The complaints of the Boston distillers had some foundation in fact. In Rhode Island there was certainly distilling at Newport as early as 1729,[2] and forty years later there were '10 distill houses which are employed the most part of the year and 3 more, that distill occasionally'.[3] It was sometimes worth while for Boston merchants to send molasses round to Newport to be distilled.[4] At Providence there were distilleries well before the middle of the eighteenth century. At New York, by 1738, there were two.[5] (The alarmist Barbadians believed there were sixteen, entirely supplied with French molasses.[6]) The New York distillers prided themselves on the belief that their rum was a cut above that of New England. So did those of Philadelphia, whose coy beginnings, about 1700, are thus described

[1] *Boston Record Commission, Report no. 121: Boston Town Records, 1742–1757*, pp. 100, 221, 238.

[2] Deposition of John Browne, distiller, Newport, 5 September 1739, in *R.I.H.S. Magazine*, xi, 8. (This document gives some interesting information about the terms of employment.)

[3] Christopher Champlin to Colin Drummond, 29 May 1769, in Mason's *Newport*, 'inlaid edition', R.I.H.S.

[4] John Powell, Boston, to Christopher Champlin, 28 May 1764, 'Letters of Boston Merchants, 1732–66', Boston Public Library, MSS. I, i, 2, p. 5.

[5] Archibald Kennedy, Collector of Customs, New York, to Board of Trade, 18 January 1737/8, *N.Y.Col.Doc.*, vi, 127.

[6] Governor Worsley to Board of Trade, 26 March 1723, *Calendar of State Papers, America and West Indies, 1721–3*, no. 486.

by Isaac Norris: 'I could not gett all Bbds rum therefore bought some of J^no Budd made of melass here and mixt it. I think it only wants age to taste well and is strong enough'; and later, 'people give 5/6 here for Bbds rum when that wch is made from melass here is offer'd, for the sp^t may be really fine and good yet it is not the right rum stink'.[1] By 1731 it was being assumed, at any rate by Pennsylvanians, that their distilleries supplied the Virginia and Newfoundland markets.[2] In the prices current after 1750 Philadelphia rum was usually a penny or twopence better in the home market than that of New England. Further south, William Lux writes in 1764 as if the first distillery had lately been started at Baltimore.[3] Of Charleston, South Carolina, we learn that the still-houses had in 1768 'a run'—collectively, it is to be presumed—'of 6 hhd a day'.[4]

The dispersion of the distilling industry, like that of the West India trade itself, was favoured by local jealousies and local legislation. The Connecticut laws already cited must have incidentally favoured Connecticut's own distilleries. In some other colonies laws were openly passed for this purpose: thus Nova Scotia was said in 1772 to have laid a heavy duty on all foreign spirits imported, in order to favour the Halifax distilleries,[5] and Rhode Island had an Act of 1731 'for the laying a duty upon sugar manufactured in the neighbouring governments, and imported into this colony'.

This attempt to reserve for a particular community the profits of industrialization, so characteristic of the mercantilism of the time, sometimes appears in a less easily recognizable form. It got mixed up with the question of control of quality in the celebrated controversy over the Bolting Act of New York. Governors Dongan and Fletcher confirmed, to the mayor and

---

[1] I.N. to Richard Hill, 25 March 1702; to P. Chardon, 20 April 1702, Isaac Norris Letter-Book, i, 397, 400, H.S.P.

[2] *Calendar of State Papers, America and West Indies, 1731*, no. 561.

[3] 'The sale of molasses is dull however as we have a distillery erected here I hope it will help it.' (W.L. to R. C. Carrington, 1 December 1764, Letter-Book of William Lux, N.Y.H.S.)

[4] George Champlin to Christopher Champlin, 13 December 1768, printed in *Commerce of Rhode Island*, i, 258.

[5] Hugh Finlay, Quebec, to Samuel Cary, 18 January 1772 (Box i, Mass. H.S., Samuel Cary MSS.).

Common Council of the city, in 1684 and 1694, a supposed
sole right of bolting flour for export. Fletcher cancelled this
privilege in 1694, at the instance of the country constituencies,
and the city authorities kicked up a very great fuss.[1] They
claimed that the quality and reputation of New York flour was
lowered by the unskilfulness of the country bolters; and this
appears to have been true, for the price of New York flour,
which was higher than that of Philadelphia flour both before
and afterwards, was several shillings below it just at this time.[2]
But this was not the whole story, for the city interests also complained that the country bolter engrossed the country corn, the
city bolter had to move into the country to get at it, and the
city cooper went with him.[3] The city interests revenged themselves by taxing all flour brought out of the country—a measure
which had nothing to do with control of quality. Later, the
legislature of New Jersey, a province economically tributary to
New York, laid a duty on all wheat exported, in order to
encourage the bolting of flour among themselves.[4]

The same conflict over the possession of an industrial process
appears in another form. The West Indian agitation which
brought about the Molasses Act in 1733 had a number of
different motives;[5] undoubtedly one of them was the indignation with which the planters saw themselves deprived of the
monopoly of distilling rum. Not every planter possessed a still
of his own; but there were some colonies, notably Barbados and
Antigua, where the molasses was normally distilled on the
plantation.[6] These were just the colonies where the agitation
for the Molasses Act began; and it is not fanciful to suggest that
the leaders of the movement had it in mind to force the North
Americans to take their rum by cutting them off from supplies
of foreign molasses. It was for this purpose that they decried
New England rum as specially unwholesome, and wrested to

[1] *Calendar of State Papers, America and West Indies, 1697-8*, no. 846, v; *1699*, nos.
769, xv, 890, 1209.
[2] *V. infra*, p. 38.
[3] Lord Cornbury to Board of Trade, 1 July 1708, *New York Col. Doc.*, v 57.
[4] *Ibid.; Calendar of State Papers, America and West Indies, 1697-8*, no. 846, v; *1699*,
no. 26; *1700*, no. 953, xxxv; *1714-15*, no. 35.
[5] I shall deal later, pp. 53-7, with the Molasses Act.
[6] In consequence, as I shall show later, home-produced molasses was only
available at these colonies occasionally and in small quantities.

their argument the humanitarian legislation of the colonies which restrained the sale of all rum to the Indians.[1] On other occasions, pamphleteers or colonial officials came near to saying that the planter had a right to sell his molasses in the form of rum.[2] The northern colonies looked upon the matter in the same light: some of their writers treated the Act as an attempt to kill the distilleries of the continent for the benefit of the islands.[3] The Act was ineffective in this as in all other respects; but it is an interesting incident in the struggle over the dispersion or concentration of the industrial processes connected with this trade. Dispersion won, as it always did; and thus, though a particular place might enjoy a quasi-monopoly or at least a pre-eminence in a particular article or process, such advantages were brief and rare. The trade retained, as a whole, a variety and a keenness of competition which must have been almost unique in the eighteenth-century world.

[1] This argument was perfectly unhistorical, for many of these laws were passed at a time when there was very little distilling in New England, and the earliest of them all expressly mentioned the unwholesomeness of West Indies rum, then a novelty (*v. supra*, pp. 29–31).

[2] Answer of the Island of Barbados to the Case for the Northern Colonies, Public Record Office, C.O. 28/22, Y 115.

[3] *Some Considerations humbly offer'd upon the Bill now depending in the House of Lords, Relating to the Trade between the Northern Colonies and the Sugar Islands. In a Letter to a Noble Peer* (reprinted in *American Weekly Mercury*, 6–13 July 1732).

CHAPTER II

THE OUTWARD CARGOES

I. THE ASSORTMENT OF CARGOES

THE cargoes in this trade were exceedingly various. Some idea of the chief articles has already been given in the table on pages 25–6. The list includes the natural products of more than a thousand miles of coast; it is no wonder that the range is great. But even a single vessel of less than a hundred tons might carry a cargo, less various indeed than that of a whole continent, but diverse enough. To take an example chosen at random: the Sloop *Mary Ann*, owned by the Browns of Providence, Rhode Island, sailed for Surinam in October 1766 with the following cargo: 100 hogsheads tobacco, 122 boxes spermaceti candles, 1,975 staves, 433 hoops, 4,000 bricks, 1,700 feet heading, 8 horses with awning (and hay, oats and water for their use), 3,500 bunches onions, 35 wood axes, 62 shaken hogsheads, 9⅔ barrels beef, 5⅔ barrels pork, 7 cwt. ship bread, 3 firkins butter, 30 oars, 12 barrels flour, 25 barrels tar, 8 barrels oil, 3 'shotes'[1] and 50 kegs oysters.[2] Even if the shook hogsheads and some of the lumber were for the cooperage of the return cargo of molasses and the beef, pork, bread and 'shotes' were ship's stores (which may well be, for there is no account of their sales), this is a mixed cargo; and more extreme examples could have been found.

There were good reasons for such variety. As I have already suggested, it might insure the shippers against the risk of glutting the tiny markets of the islands with any one article. It

---

[1] Pigs.

[2] Papers of Sloop *Mary Ann*, 1772, Brown MSS., J.C.B.L. The variety of Rhode Island cargoes was no new thing: Felix-Christian Spöri, in a Dutch ship which touched at the colony in 1661, noted that she was loaded there with lumber for cask, salt meat, flour, bread, and 30 fine horses, for whom hay was shipped, twisted up into ropes so as to save space. (F. C. Spöri, *Americanische Reiss-beschreibung nach den Caribes Inseln und Neu England* (Zürich, 1677), p. 44.)

37

also resulted, in part, from the haphazard way in which these
export cargoes were collected—a point to which I shall have to
return shortly.[1] It was more noticeable in some ports than in
others. The example I have quoted comes from Rhode Island,
a colony with only one staple product (horses) and no definite
hinterland. The merchants of Rhode Island had to collect the
materials for a cargo as best they could from the surrounding
farmers, from their own few manufactures, from the fishermen
of Nantucket, from any other passer-by or coastwise speculator
in goods fit for the West India market. The same thing is true
of Boston, a commercial capital whose merchants drew upon
the resources of widespread farms, forests and fisheries. It was
even true, though to a less degree, of Philadelphia and New
York: these commercial centres collected the miscellaneous
products of the neighbouring provinces, but they also had their
own characteristic manufactures of bread and flour, which
bulked larger in their West India cargoes than any one thing
Boston or Newport had to show. Other ports were still more
specialized: some of the Virginia rivers exported very little
besides lumber; Piscataqua, Salem and Marblehead little but
lumber and fish. Of course, there was fish and fish: many
invoices, especially in the later years, specified mackerel, ale-
wives, menhaden and so forth. Still, one could not mistake the
relatively homogeneous Salem cargoes for the very miscellaneous ones which the Bostonians and Newport men carried to
the West Indies.

Not much was said about the competition between different
provinces in the production of similar articles. Comparisons
were quite often drawn between the flour of Philadelphia and
that of New York.[2] The pork of New Jersey and that of the

---

[1] *V. infra,* p. 41.

[2] In 1699 Isaac Norris of Philadelphia wrote that 'our flower is sometimes 2 or
3s. in a hundred or more dearer yn New York yet . . . its proportion of fines will
bear it'. (I.N. to Job Williams, 1 August 1699, Letter-Books of Isaac Norris, i, 38,
H.S.P.) This was just at the time when, according to the New York controversialists, the bolting of flour in that colony was in the hands of unskilled practitioners
who lowered the quality by mixing Indian corn with the wheat (*v. supra,* p. 35).
Fifty years later the boot was on the other leg: David Fogo wrote from Antigua,
27 September 1755, to John Reynell: 'the New York flour when at markett outsells
your flour above 5/- in the hundred, their middling is by much prefferable to your
finest or best sort' (Coates-Reynell Papers, Box xi, H.S.P.).

Southern colonies were held to compete: the latter was badly prepared at first, and always inferior to the best Burlington pork: but it was cheaper, and thought good enough for the Negroes. The hucksters of the Leeward Islands (who presumably dealt with the Negroes) were said to prefer it to the better article, which was only wanted for the private consumption of the planters' families.[1] But comparisons such as these were not made often. The production of the continent was too little standardized, and the local diversities too slight and indefinable. On the other hand, the planters were, for the most part, supplying their slaves' wants rather than their own, and were therefore the less nice in their choice. They bought from hand to mouth, and if they ever aimed at a bargain in the purchase of these coarse goods, it was price rather than quality that attracted them.

A few curiosities in this trade are worth mention. In two articles—tobacco and refined sugar—the northern colonies might be regarded as carrying coals to Newcastle. Barbados was originally a tobacco colony, yet we find a Boston merchant carrying tobacco thither as early as 1672.[2] In the British West Indies sugar was already replacing tobacco, which was imported not only from Virginia but from much further north: that of Connecticut and Rhode Island cannot have been very agreeable, but somebody—presumably the slaves—must have found it good enough to smoke. The export of refined sugar to the West Indies is not really as surprising as it looks: for the British planters (perhaps discouraged by the heavy import duty of 1685 in England) hardly ever attempted to refine their own outside Barbados, where a semi-manufacture known as clayed sugar was still produced. Northern refiners such as John van Cortlandt were therefore able to dispose of some of

---

[1] 'Pork is now wanted, but what is shipt from your port is not altogether so suitable for huxters as what comes from Virginia and Carolina' (Birkett and Booth, Antigua, to John Reynell, *ibid.*, Box iv). 'As to pork it is always saleable and the Virginia Merryland or North Carolina pork will sell within 4 or 5/- per barrel as much as the best Philadelphia or New York unless it be a few barrels for some private family's uses. Since last April I have sold between 3 and 400 barrels pork wch was very near all sold to the hucksters of this town' (John Watkins, St. Kitts, to Thomas Clifford, Clifford Correspondence, vol. i, no. 222, H.S.P.).

[2] *Records of the Courts of Assistants, Colony of the Massachusetts Bay*, iii, 246.

their product in the British sugar colonies. One must, however, admire his enterprise or his ignorance in consigning refined sugars to Martinique, for many French planters refined their own to a high degree.[1]

One other article of export was much discussed at the time. When the British sugar-planters began to conceive a jealousy of the trade which the North Americans carried on to the French, Dutch and Spanish colonies, they accused them of exporting money there (always a heavy offence against the mercantilist canon of economic propriety) either directly or by carrying to the foreign islands the proceeds of goods sold in the British.[2] In the correspondence of the northern merchants there is little trace of either of these practices; but on the few occasions when the export of money to the West Indies is mentioned it is usually the foreign islands that the writer had in mind.[3] When scarcity did not oblige the French authorities to admit British cargoes of provisions, money might be their only inducement to allow the trade at all.[4] Perhaps, moreover, the French currency regulations gave some encouragement to the introduction of light coins which would not have passed current elsewhere. The Browns of Providence tried a venture of this sort to Hispaniola in 1772, with very disagreeable results.

'What we shall do with the light gould', their captain wrote, 'I don't know, for Peter [the supercargo] won't lay a copers worth out since Capt. —— sising for the same sort and his vesel and cargo confisticated and the french marchant and all the Inglish men that was on bord are all in clost jail and what to due with it I dont no for thare so particler about takeing of gold that they

[1] John van Cortlandt to David Purviance, Martinique, 15 December 1762, Letter-Book of John van Cortlandt, N[ew] Y[ork] P[ublic] L[ibrary].

[2] Answer of the Leeward Islands and Jamaica to the Case of the Northern Colonies, Public Record Office, C.O. 152/19, T. 122.

[3] For example, Philip Cuyler wrote to his father, 3 December 1759, 'I am concerned a quarter in a flag truce will sail in about ten days or twelve to Port au Prince and gold is not to be had in town which is the only good thing to send as provisions of all kinds is prohibited', so he asks for 100 half-johannes (a Portuguese gold coin) by return of post. (Letter-Book of Philip Cuyler, N.Y.P.L.)

[4] 'Nothing but money will answer here and nothing will obtain a permitt so soon' (Samuel Haynes, Fort Dauphin, to Thomas Fayerweather, 4 August 1763, Fayerweather MSS., N.E. Hist. and Gen. Soc.). G. G. Beekman seems to have sent moidores to Barbados in 1766 (see his letter to Willet Taylor, 10 February 1766, N.Y.H.S.).

way it all and if they find it to be short of wait thay will take it away from you and keep it.'[1]

The cargoes exported from North America to the islands were collected in a number of ways. Many of them, especially in the more primitive times and places, resulted from a system of local barter. The exporters of northern produce were also the importers of sugar, molasses and rum, which they sold to store-keepers or to consumers for 'country pay', often of the most miscellaneous character. There was only one way to turn this stuff to account—to export it to the West Indies; and this fact probably explains, better than anything else, the great variety of the outward cargoes to which I have already referred.

In the greater ports, however, the merchants assorted their cargoes somewhat more scientifically. Although their papers reveal more coastwise speculation in West India produce than in goods for the West India market, the latter is not wholly absent. They drew to themselves the lumber and foodstuffs of the adjoining provinces, and this enabled them to assort their West India cargoes not only better but quicker. The Governor of Maryland complained in 1762 that much of that colony's wheat and flour was carried to Philadelphia,

> the price there being always higher than in Maryland owing to the vast trade carried on from thence to the West Indies & other parts; as the merchants there can always load their vessels at once they can afford to give more for the cargoes than merchants in this province can give, because ours must be a long time collecting a cargo for even a small vessel there being no town or port in Maryland where any considerable quantity of country produce can be purchased at once or altogether.[2]

This was before the rise of Baltimore.

Few of the trades which supplied these goods had any definite organization. The exporter of lumber had, at least, some responsibility for assorting his cargo: since every plantation would require a due proportion of staves, hoops and heading in its casks, and those which distilled their molasses would

[1] William Bradford to Nicholas Brown and Co., 3 and 7 February 1773, papers of Sloop "A", Brown MSS., J.C.B.L.

[2] Sharpe to Calvert, 25 September 1762 (*Maryland Archives, Correspondence of Governor Sharpe*, iii, 72).

need some white oak for their rum puncheons along with the red oak for the sugar hogsheads.[1] He might have to fetch the lumber himself: according to the custom of Piscataqua in 1663, it was the receiver's duty, not the sawyer's, to bring the rafts of boards ashore, as they came down the river.[2] Even if he found the lumber brought to his door, he might have to store it some months, for the best exporting season did not coincide with the sawing season when the sap was down; and he might improve this interval by having the staves shaved so as to take up less room in the ships. Contracts for sawing may have been made sometimes, but they were usually proposed by West Indians, anxious to make sure of their supplies; the merchants of Philadelphia seem to have preferred buying in the open market.[3] The flour trade seems to have been organized in a very rudimentary way. Most of the mills were up-country (hence we hear, in Philadelphia, of 'wagon flour' and 'shallop flour'— the latter less esteemed because likely to have got wet in transit). They sometimes worked by contract, but these contracts usually seem to have been given at the seasons when a West India market was assured; at such times, casual buyers were likely to find all the flour pre-engaged.[4]

Little attempt was made to control the quality of these exports. I have already mentioned the controversy over the attempts to maintain the quality of New York flour by confining the right of bolting to the city.[5] The jealousy of the city manufacturers was not entirely disinterested, but they probably had an excuse for it: the Philadelphia exporters often exclaimed, about the same time, against the inferiority of country-bolted

[1] John Reynell's correspondents in Antigua often advised him that staves would not sell so well without the due proportion of heading (said to be 1 to 4), but their accounts of sales did not always bear this out. (See the letters of Birkett and Booth, 13 November 1752, David Fogo, 5 September 1754, 27 January 1754–5, Coates-Reynell Papers, Boxes vii, viii, ix, H.S.P.)

[2] *Essex County, Records and Files of the Quarterly Court*, iii, 92.

[3] Isaac Norris to Thomas Raby, 17 June 1703, Letter-Books of Isaac Norris, ii, 59, H.S.P.; Jonathan Dickinson to Isaac Gale, 28 April 1718, Letter-Book of Jonathan Dickinson, p. 186, L.C.P.; Bayly, Elworthy and Bayly, to John Reynell, 13 April, 3 June, 10 October 1754, Coates-Reynell Papers, Box viii, H.S.P.; Nathaniel Donnell to John Reynell, 11 May 1754, *ibid.*

[4] S. and J. Smith to Nathaniel Holmes, 24 August 1765, Letter-Book of S. and J. Smith, Library of Congress; to Thomas Boylston, 17 September 1765, *ibid.*

[5] *V. supra*, pp. 34–5.

flour.[1] Exports of lumber were subject to inspection in more than one colony. A Massachusetts law of 1646 must positively have encouraged the export of thin and inferior boards to the West Indies, for it only provided for the inspection of exports to Spain and Portugal;[2] but other New England laws were more general, and may even have been provoked by complaints from the West Indies, where there was some talk of regulating imports.[3] A New York law of 1741 attempted to maintain the reputation of the colony's pork and beef in the West Indies by preventing abuses in repacking.[4] It is not clear whether such phrases as 'Surinam horses' or 'Jamaica fish' connoted any definite specifications of quality. The former was in common use at Rhode Island, but I have not been able to discover whether it meant a bad or a middling horse: since the horses were shipped in order to comply with an edict of the Surinam government, admitting foreign traders only if they brought horses, they are unlikely to have been good ones.[5] As for 'Jamaica fish', it was a very general term, and fish under this denomination was often shipped to Madeira and the Canaries.[6]

Branded goods were not unheard of in this trade, but there are very few instances. Perhaps the best-known is that of the United Company of Spermaceti Chandlers, whose candles were sold all over the West Indies after the Seven Years War.[7] In 1766 G. G. Beekman exported two tons of 'Hackets best iron,

[1] 'As to wt thou says of our flour all tradrs of note are very much concerned for the reputation of the place, & while the bolting was in good men's hands in this town wee made generally a good comodity but now tis spread all over the country & every farmer almost bolts his own that it is in so many hands that as yet wee can come to no remedie' (Isaac Norris to Clement Plumsted, 1 July 1709, Isaac Norris Letter-Book, v, 45, H.S.P.). In 1717 or 1718 Elizabeth Hill of Philadelphia, consigning some flour to William Morris, told him, 'The flower is of the town bolting & therefore I expect it will bring the price of the finest flower' (*Colden Papers, N.Y.H.S. Collections*, 1917, i, 40).

[2] *Records of the Colony of Massachusetts Bay* (ed. Shurtleff, Boston, 1853), ii, 169.

[3] *Connecticut Public Records*, i, 59; C.O. 1/53, nos. 4 (Leeward Islands), 12, ii (New Hampshire).

[4] Lt. Govr. Clarke to Board of Trade, 22 April 1741, *N.Y. Col. Doc.*, vi, 185.

[5] The Dutch edict of 1704 was still in force in Surinam in 1767, when it was recited in an official notification which is found among the Brown MSS., J.C.B.L.

[6] William Cawthorne, Madeira, to Thomas Fayerweather, 24 February 1763, Thomas Fayerweather Commercial Papers, N.E.H. and G.S.

[7] A reproduction of their trade mark is given by the late Mr. Worthington C. Ford in *The Commerce of Rhode Island, 1725–1800*, i, 305.

which is in esteem at Barbadose'.[1] A letter which John Reynell received from Antigua in 1754 seems to show that different brands of flour were still known there: he was advised to ship 'of the best marks you can get, such as ⓘⓦ, ⓘⓣ, Spring mill, Paterson's or Ricketts, but procure as many of the best marks as you can, they are but little inferior to Soper's 10 at Albany'. A little later there is evidence of branded flour in Maryland.[2] Hopkins's ship bread, from Philadelphia, is also singled out for mention.[3]

For deciding what and when to ship, or whether to ship at all, the exporters relied above all on the news and advice they received from the markets. There were so many markets, and the news from them conflicted so much, that it cannot often have had a perceptible influence on the price of export goods in the northern ports, unless it was of so general a sort—a hurricane or a campaign—that its meaning could not be mistaken. Nevertheless, in the earlier, simpler days, when Barbados still weighed almost as much as all the other colonies together, and little news travelled from one northern port to another, flour might rise or fall a few shillings in price at Philadelphia or New York in response to the demand of a single colony.[4] In later years the correspondence between the principal towns was much closer, and exporters eagerly collected news, not only of ships in the islands, but of departures, actual or impending, from the continent. Such a flow of news from so many sources must have tended to reduce the fluctuations of price at a particular port. The newspapers must have helped to disseminate this commercial information. Perhaps not all their news was

---

[1] G. G. Beekman to Willet Taylor, 10 February 1766, Letter-Book of G. G. Beekman, N.Y.H.S.

[2] N. Booth, Antigua, to J. Reynell, 21 May 1754, Coates-Reynell Papers, Box viii, H.S.P.; David Fogo to J. Reynell, 27 September 1755, *ibid.*, Box ix; William Lux to Darby Lux, 10 March 1764, Letter-Book of William Lux, N.Y.H.S.

[3] David Fogo to J. Reynell, 27 September 1755, Coates-Reynell Papers, Box ix, H.S.P.

[4] Isaac Norris to Joseph Coysgarne, 21 June 1700, Isaac Norris Letter-Book, i, 185, H.S.P. These fluctuations must have had an after-effect of another kind: if the news of the markets for North American goods in the West Indies was bad, fewer ships would go from the continent and, a little later, fewer would return with West India produce, so that its price would rise, a few months later, on the continent.

given in good faith: Nicholas Brown advised his brother in 1764 that 'if a stroke was put in the Newport paper truly giveing a state of the rum trade upon the coast of Ginea it may prevent many vessels from pushg that way this fall' and, incidentally, lower the price of tobacco which the Browns wanted to buy. 'This', he added, 'is a subject worth our attention a small matter as 2 dols will get it from the Newport into the Boston and York papers, or Phil^a'.[1]

This was as far as the exporters could usually go towards keeping each other out of the market. With so many ports to start from and so many small markets to supply, combination was almost impossible. Only one instance of it is on record: at various times from 1766 to 1772, a handful of merchants in Rhode Island (the Browns of Providence in the lead) tried hard to corner the export of Rhode Island tobacco to the Dutch colony of Surinam. This scheme had, at one time or another, all the characteristics of a modern cartel. Fixed proportions of the trade were allotted to the participating firms; at one time the sales in Surinam were put under a single management, at another the proceeds of the several cargoes were to be pooled and divided. At least once, though apparently not always, the price to be paid to the tobacco-planters in Rhode Island was fixed by solemn agreement; the participants naturally had to buy up all the tobacco that offered, and on one occasion they found themselves forced to take much more than they had originally intended; in order to make sure of their monopoly, they even empowered their agents in Surinam to buy any free tobacco that might arrive there, for example from Connecticut. This enterprise appears to have been an expensive failure, though no balance sheet has been found. It could only have been attempted in a rather peculiar article and the trade of a small and remote Caribbean colony. Perhaps it was no accident that this project originated in Rhode Island, whose monopolistic tendencies were already exhibited in the rudimentary spermaceti candle trust.[2]

---

[1] Nicholas Brown to Moses Brown, 12 September 1764, Moses Brown Papers, 60, R.I.H.S.

[2] A fuller account of this scheme may be found in James B. Hedges, *The Browns of Providence Plantations* (New Haven, 1952), pp. 31–8.

By no means all the cargoes for the West Indies started from the home port of the ship and her owner. From the first, there were many voyages from New England to Barbados via the wine islands of the Atlantic or the slave coast of Africa, where the most important part of the cargo was picked up. Thus in December 1649 the *Fortune* was to sail from Charlestown to Barbados by way of Guinea.[1] In November 1659 a ketch owned by merchants in Madeira and Barbados carried lumber from Piscataqua river to Madeira, whence she went to Barbados.[2] In 1668 we hear of a most complicated voyage, Boston–Barbados–Boston–Madeira–Barbados–Boston[3] and so forth. *This is complicated?*

Probably these roundabout voyages were commoner in the early times than they became at the end of the seventeenth century, for the London merchants, with their interests and connections all over the Atlantic, held the system of commerce together at first. But at all times a roundabout voyage had much to recommend it; above all, a voyage to the wine islands. The vineyards offered a market for the New England lumber, also, especially at crop-time, for the New England fish.[4] The same ship would carry forward to the West Indies the inferior wine which nobody but the planters would drink,[5] with the somewhat better qualities which found a market in North America and were said to improve on the voyage. The proceeds of the wine sold in the West Indies would buy a load of rum or sugar home.[6] A slave voyage had many of the same advantages, though it was not until the eighteenth century that the Rhode Islanders rediscovered for themselves the art, familiar to the Barbadians in the seventeenth, of buying their slaves for the West India market with rum distilled from West India molasses. Lastly, the merchants of the northern and middle colonies sent their vessels to the agricultural south to

[1] *Aspinwall Notarial Records*, p. 411.

[2] *Essex County, Records and Files of the Quarterly Court*, ii, 203.

[3] *Suffolk Deeds*, vi, 65.

[4] William Cawthorne to Thomas Fayerweather, 24 February 1763, Thomas Fayerweather Commercial Papers, N.E.H. and G.S.

[5] *Ibid.*; Stephens, Porter and Co., Madeira, to J. Reynell, 8 May 1748, Coates-Reynell Papers, Box v, H.S.P.

[6] Isaac Norris to G. McKenzie, 9 October 1704, Isaac Norris Letter-Book, ii, 213, H.S.P.

buy lumber, pork or Indian corn for the West Indies. Here, too, a *perpetuum mobile* could be established—with the produce of Virginia or Carolina, molasses could be bought, carried to Boston or Philadelphia, there distilled into rum and returned to Virginia or Carolina to buy another cargo of local produce for the West Indies.[1]

II. THE CHOICE OF MARKETS

About the choice of markets in the West Indies it is almost impossible to say anything definite or consistent. Each of the colonial ports traded, in more or less degree, with each of the islands. At a particular time and in a particular port, one island might be preferred to another: according to John Watts, the connoisseurs of New York preferred St. Kitts to other West India markets, and had so little communication with Barbados that it was quicker to send a letter there by way of Philadelphia.[2] But such statistics as we have, show that neither of these things had been true in earlier times; on the contrary, Barbados and Antigua had been much frequented by New Yorkers for the West India rum of which they imported so much. Very likely they were not true even in Watts's own time: merchants' generalizations, uttered on the spur of the moment, were not worth much. Statistics are a safer guide; but unfortunately those we have are few, mostly for unrepresentative years, and mean little without interpretation.

Between 1 January 1701 and 31 July 1703, 110 vessels brought West India produce into the port of New York; of these, 23 came from Barbados, 10 from Antigua, 3 from St. Kitts, 7 from Nevis, 25 from Jamaica, 11 from Surinam and Essequibo, 1 from St. Domingue, 1 from St. Thomas, 2 from Salt Tortuga, 2 from Bermuda, and 25 from Boston or other New England ports.[3]

The clearances of shipping from three principal ports

---

[1] There are instances of this in the letter-book of Robert Ellis (H.S.P.). Ellis was primarily an importer of slaves from the West Indies, but he was just as ready to import rum or sugar.

[2] *Letter-Book of John Watts* (*N.Y.H.S. Collections*, lxi), pp. 113, 364.

[3] New York, Hall of Records, Old Conveyances, Lib. 30.

between 24 June 1714 and 24 June 1717 were divided as follows:[1]

	Boston		Salem		New York	
	Vessels	Tons	Vessels	Tons	Vessels	Tons
British sugar islands	495	27,831	59	2,296	250	8,776
Foreign plantations	58	2,597	—	—	85	2,585
Surinam	—	—	2	75	—·	—
'West Indies'	23	1,335	10	304	—	—
Bay of Campeche	25	1,675	—	—	—	—
Total, all destinations	1247	62,788	232	13,431	645	22,392

The clearances and entries in the West India trade for December 1729 to 4 December 1730 were printed in the *Boston Weekly Newsletter*, 4 March 1730/1.[2] Those which concern us are reproduced on the opposite page.

This list requires some commentary. In the first place the clearances, especially from Boston, for the British sugar colonies exceed the entries. This excess is general, for many ships were built for sale abroad. The large excess of clearances for the 'West Indies' is explained by the very common habit of giving the master discretionary orders to sell at whatever market he found best; he would not know which particular island he was clearing for, but he must know, and usually chose (before the imposition of the duty on foreign molasses) to say from whence he had returned. The excess of clearances for Barbados and Jamaica can likewise be explained. Barbados was the windwardmost island; it was an easy market to sell at, for the population was large and wholesale business was relatively well organized; lastly, there was frequent news of the markets to leeward. For all these reasons owners often instructed their captains to touch first at Barbados but only to sell if it seemed to be the best thing to do. The excess of clearances for Barbados is balanced by the excess of entries from the

---

[1] Board of Trade, State of the British Plantations, 8 September 1721, printed in *N.Y. Col. Doc.*, v, 618.

[2] There are also figures for a slightly later period in the *American Weekly Mercury*, 16 March 1731/2.

		Boston	Salem and New Hamp-shire	Rhode Island	New York	Phila-delphia
For or from:						
Antigua	C	7	3	8	18	14
	E	13	4	12	11	14
Barbados	C	34	13	25	23	29
	E	19	20	23	14	17
Cap François	C	—	—	—	—	—
	E	11	—	—	—	—
Curaçao	C	1	—	—	29	2
	E	3	—	—	12	—
Cayenne	C	11	—	—	—	—
	E	4	—	—	—	—
St. Eustatius	C	—	—	—	—	—
	E	3	—	—	—	—
Guadeloupe	C	—	—	—	—	—
	E	4	—	—	—	—
Honduras	C	—	—	—	—	—
	E	17	—	—	—	—
Jamaica	C	47	2	17	23	25
	E	23	—	23	30	17
Leeward Islands	C	20	—	3	—	—
	E	—	—	—	—	—
New Providence	C	—	—	—	—	—
(Bahamas)	E	—	—	3	—	—
St. Kitts	C	17	—	—	—	9
	E	1	—	9	—	12
St. Thomas	C	—	—	—	—	—
	E	—	—	3	—	—
Surinam	C	14	—	11	—	4
	E	24	—	8	3	3
Tortuga	C	—	—	—	—	—
	E	—	6	—	—	—
West Indies	C	49	16	14	—	—
	E	—	5	—	—	—

foreign islands and from Salt Tortuga, for the salt fleets were made up at Barbados but did not usually touch there again on the way home. The figures for Jamaica can be explained in much the same way. Kingston was a good market for northern produce, especially while the South Sea Company's factors

E

resided there to further the trade with the Spanish colonies; but some Bostonians who had sold in Jamaica evidently preferred to take in their homeward cargoes of molasses in the French port of Cap François, and still more went across to the settlements on the coast of Honduras for a cargo of logwood which they brought home to Boston or perhaps carried straight to Europe.

These figures, collected just before the Molasses Act introduced a new incentive to falsification, probably show fairly enough how far the trade with the foreign colonies had grown at that time. This question was much discussed by pamphleteers, and the choice whether to trade with the British or the foreign colonies was at all times one of the most momentous which the merchants had to make.

Very few of them can have had much to do with the foreign colonies before the end of the seventeenth century; and what intercourse they had, was unlike that which developed in the eighteenth. New York retained, from its Dutch origin, a particularly close connexion with Curaçao (this is still visible in the figures quoted above) and Boston and Philadelphia too had some trade with the Dutch and Danish settlements which, even if not neutral in the great French wars, chose to behave as if they had been. Purist judges and customs officers like Randolph and Quary often complained of this trade; but the gravamen of their charges was the smuggling of European goods into North America, and the merchants defended themselves by alleging that they brought in money—neither accusers nor accused said much about the importation of foreign sugars.[1] The one exception was the Dutch colony of Surinam, from which, it seems, some rum and molasses was already coming in. So well established must this intercourse with Surinam have appeared by 1715 that when the Government began to think of stopping the trade with the French islands, Jonathan Dickinson of Philadelphia exclaimed, with an air of injured surprise, 'Wee have the trade with Suranam for mellossos and

---

[1] *Calendar of State Papers, America and West Indies, 1697–8*, nos. 45, 768; *1700*, no. 100. Isaac Norris, who was concerned in a vessel bound for Curaçao, ordered the supercargo to sell for money or negroes if cheap, and to return to Nevis in order to buy a cargo of sugar. (I.N. to Jeffery Pinnell, 20 July 1699, Isaac Norris Letter-Book, i, 38, H.S.P.)

why not with the other?'[1] The molasses of Surinam was 'ordinary', but it could be bought for 3d. the gallon when Barbados molasses was 12d. to 15d. and Barbados rum 2s.; 'therefore,' said Dickinson,

> the Surinam trade will live when our islanders may starve for the Dutch neither use their molasses nor their rum, save what they give to their negroes but we are their only customers for molasses & of late rum, considerable quantitys come from thence, they take to grinding their damaged canes & work it up & sell it for about 6d per gallon. . . . We purchase a whole load there of rum & molasses for a few sorry jades of horses which they buy up here at 40/- and 50/- per head and half a score such may load a sloop as big as my sloop Mary that was.[2]

Perhaps it was the French wars that caused Surinam to remain alone so long as a source of supply, for very few North Americans had the hardihood, so early as this, to trade with an enemy, though some American flour was said to have reached the French islands through the neutral Danes.[3] Perhaps, too, the brisk trade with the pirates kept the exports to the foreign sugar colonies from developing, by providing an alternative outlet for northern produce in the days of Captain Kidd.[4] But after the Peace of Utrecht the French islands' sugar production developed with a sudden bound, and the North Americans began to flock to them for the by-products of their sugar mills. The town of Boston preserved, in 1753, a tradition that the distillery of foreign molasses into rum had begun 'about forty years since'; this tradition was correct to the year.[5]

[1] Jonathan Dickinson to Isaac Gale, 2 May 1715 (Letter-Book of Jonathan Dickinson, p. 23, L.C.P.).

[2] Jonathan Dickinson to Isaac Gale, 10 May 1721, *ibid.*, p. 379. Dickinson's attitude is interesting, for he had a plantation in Jamaica but lived as a merchant in Philadelphia. On the whole, he thought on this subject as a Philadelphian: he saw no harm in trying to trade with the French at Leogane, and endeavoured to induce his Jamaican friends and relatives to take a part in his plans.

[3] Cadwallader Colden's account of the trade of New York, transmitted to the Board of Trade, 25 June 1723, printed in *N.Y. Col. Doc.*, v, 685.

[4] William Penn in 1700 accused the neighbouring colonies of having earned a million in the last ten years by selling flour to pirates. (*Calendar of State Papers, America and West Indies, 1700*, no. 366.) If this is anything like true, they would not have had much to spare for the French and Dutch sugar colonies.

[5] Petition of the Town to the Lieut. Governor and General Court, 20 May 1753, *Boston Town Records, 1742–1757, Boston Record Commission, Report no. 14*, p. 238.

The complaints of British customs officials and sugar-planters rose in a sudden spate. Within a year or two they tried to induce the Government to put a stop to the trade by invoking an Anglo-French treaty of 1686. This only issued in orders which had no real legal meaning; for it was clear that the treaty only empowered each government to arrest trespassing ships belonging to subjects of the other; there were very few French trespassers for the British authorities to arrest, and the French authorities did not usually choose to arrest the British trespassers.[1] About the same time, in some of the British sugar islands the legislatures took the matter into their own hands. They passed laws forbidding or penalizing the importation of foreign sugar, rum and molasses into their own ports.[2] There is no means of telling how much French produce had thus leaked into the British colonies and been carried to other parts of the empire as British: probably the volume had not been great in the French wars or earlier, but it may now have swelled quickly after the peace. Many people questioned the wisdom of such laws. If the North American captains could be sure of a plentiful supply of molasses, British or foreign, at the ports of Barbados or Jamaica, they would come there to sell their cargoes, plenty would be assured, and the local merchants would obtain the middleman's profit. Perhaps further, less definable advantages would result from making the British colonies the 'staples' for the produce of the French.[3] These advantages would be lost for the sake of a protection which would not succeed in protecting the British planter; for the North Americans who could not get French produce at the British sugar islands would seek it at the fountainhead, and take their cargoes of provisions and lumber there too. Experience showed these arguments to be true; most of these laws had to

[1] *Calendar of State Papers, America and West Indies, 1716–17*, nos. 463, 524, 571; *1717–18*, no. 598.

[2] The Barbados Act of 1715 imposed import duties of 18d. on each gallon of molasses and 2s. on each gallon of rum imported from foreign colonies. This act had little effect: in the *Case* of the Northern colonies reprinted in the *American Weekly Mercury*, 15–22 July 1731, it is alleged that most of the molasses imported by New Englanders from Barbados is of French origin.

[3] The printed 'Case of the *British* Northern Colonies', December 1731, C.O. 28/22, Y. 113; see also the other printed 'Case of the *British* Northern Colonies', C.O. 5/4, fo. 260.

be repealed, others remained without effect. The planters came to the conclusion that a stronger and more comprehensive remedy must be found.

This remedy was the celebrated and useless Molasses Act of 1733. The agitation and manœuvres which led to its passage have been so well described that it does not seem necessary to repeat the description here.[1] I shall confine myself to discussing the arguments for and against this interference with the trade.

Some of these arguments were mere attempts to create prejudice. Such, for example, were the denunciations of the sugar-planters' luxury and profligacy.[2] Such too, on the other side, were the solemn warnings against the inferior quality of the New England rum, with which the Indians were not merely debauched but killed—West India rum, apparently, was innocent of these crimes.[3] Such too, perhaps, was the charge that the North Americans carried money directly to the French or denuded the British sugar islands of cash by exporting the proceeds of their cargoes and investing them in French molasses.[4] There is so little proof of this in the merchants' papers that it must have been a rarity; the planters probably knew that, but the charge of exporting money was such a damaging one in those days that they were naturally tempted to make the most of it.

There were more serious accusations than these. I have already suggested[5] that the planters who distilled their molasses into rum did not like to see the North Americans supply themselves elsewhere with molasses which furnished employment for their distilleries. No doubt West India rum would have fetched a better price everywhere if the cheaper, though nastier, New England rum had not competed with it. The planters claimed

[1] F. W. Pitman, *The Development of the British West Indies, 1760–1763* (New Haven, 1917), chapter xi.

[2] The printed 'Case of the *British* Northern Colonies', December 1731, C.O. 28/22, Y. 113.

[3] Article in the *Daily Post Boy*, 6 March 1731/2, reprinted in the *American Weekly Mercury*, 27 July–3 August 1732.

[4] Answer of the Leeward Islands and Jamaica to the Case of the Northern Colonies, January 1731/2, C.O. 152/19, T. 122. According to a writer in *Caribbeana*, ii, 129–30, this was still going on in 1735–6, after the Act was passed.

[5] *V. supra*, pp. 35–6.

that they could increase their production of rum indefinitely if
they could only find a market for it.[1] This may have been
true: although some British planters, especially in Jamaica, had
always sold their molasses instead of distilling it (which argues
want of enterprise or of capital), it does seem likely that the
importation of raw molasses into North America, and the con-
sequent discouragement of distilling in the islands, were much
greater after the trade with the French colonies became important. But this grievance, however strong as a motive, was
not very much used as an argument.[2] It would not have been
very easy to demonstrate why the British sugar-planters should
have a monopoly of distilling, unless one accepted their atrocity
stories about the properties of the New England liquor. Moreover, a few North American controversialists managed to
suggest that the rum of a plantation could only be increased at
the expense of its sugar, and that the planters' ulterior object
was to make sugar scarce and dear in the protected home
market, by diminishing the quantity.[3]

The planters' best card was the national sense of rivalry with
the French. This was very intense in general, but nowhere
keener than in the sugar trade, for these were the very years in
which French re-exports of sugar were increasing and British
re-exports falling off. Many people thought the British planters
had only themselves to blame for their extravagance and
inefficiency.[4] It might also have been suspected that some of
them were quite content with the home market so long as they
could keep down the refiners' agitation for foreign imports of
raw sugar. The planters, however, did not admit either of
these things. They looked elsewhere for the causes of the

[1] *Remarks upon a Book, Entituled, The Present State of the Sugar Colonies consider'd*
(London, 1731), p. 19, alleges that a gentleman of St. Christopher's had affirmed
that he made at present 2,000 gallons of rum a year but could make 20,000 gallons.

[2] Governor Worsley of Barbados to Board of Trade, 7 July 1730, C.O. 28/21,
Y. 41. See also the evidence of William Frazier and Patrick Blake, *Journals of the
House of Commons*, 23 February 1730/1.

[3] *Some Considerations humbly offer'd upon the Bill now depending in the House of Lords
Relating to the Trade between the Northern Colonies and the Sugar Islands, in a Letter to a
Noble Peer*, reprinted in *American Weekly Mercury*, 6–13 July 1732. More rum really
could be made by making less sugar (*Caribbeana* (1741), ii, 242–5).

[4] *A Letter to a Noble Peer, Relating to the Bill in favour of the Sugar-Planters* (London,
1733), pp. 15–16; *The Dispute Between the Northern Colonies and the Sugar Islands set
in a Clear View* (1732).

French success, and found it in the North American trade, which provided the French planters with cheap lumber and provisions and increased their profits by enabling them to dispose of their by-products.[1] The North Americans replied that they only sold the French what the British islands could not and, indeed, would not consume, for the worst goods of all were supplied to the French.[2] This last suggestion was probably untrue, for, though the West India quality of some goods, such as fish and tobacco, was certainly inferior to that shipped to Europe, I have never come across a clear proof that worse goods were sent to the foreign West Indies than to the British. In any case, the planters rejected the whole argument. They could not always get their lumber and foodstuffs as cheap as they liked, and suspected that they might have made better bargains if the captains could not have gone to the French. Moreover they treated the question whether they could have bought the produce sold to the French as irrelevant: the important thing, they said, was to starve out the French sugar-planters, and if the North Americans were incidentally deprived of an outlet for their goods, so much the worse for them.[3] The North Americans retorted that the French could not be starved out: deprived of provisions and lumber from British sources, they would develop their own colonies of Canada, Louisiana and Acadia, and so much good trade would be thrown away for nothing.[4] The planters were partly justified in doubting the truth of this,[5] just as they had some cause for denying the North American argument that the French planters would begin distilling their molasses into rum rather than throw it

[1] See the letter of Micajah Perry to Cadwallader Colden, 27 December 1731, in *Colden Papers* (N.Y.H.S.), ii, 46–7; *Remarks upon a Book, Entituled, The Present State of the Sugar Colonies consider'd*, pp. 15–17.

[2] Printed 'Case of the *British* Northern Colonies', December 1731, C.O. 28/22, Y. 113. A similar assertion was made about the export of horses from Rhode Island in 1764. (R.I.H.S., Moses Brown Papers, Miscellanea, i, 12–13.)

[3] *The Importance of the Sugar Colonies to Great Britain Stated, and some Objections against the Sugar Colony Bill answer'd* (London, 1731), pp. 9–12.

[4] The printed 'Case of the *British* Northern Colonies', December 1731, C.O. 28/22, Y. 113; *Remarks upon a Book, Entituled, The Present State of the Sugar Colonies consider'd* (London, 1731), p. 113.

[5] *The Importance of the Sugar Colonies to Great Britain Stated, and some Objections against the Sugar Colony Bill answer'd*, pp. 12–14.

away for want of a customer[1]—it was not very likely that they could do so, for France, unlike Great Britain, had a brandy industry which was sure to demand and receive protection against rum, whatever its origin.

Finally the argument came down to the question, which group of colonies better deserved encouragement by its utility to the mother country. Each group claimed to be the better customer, but the North Americans claimed it with more fervour, because they had little other claim to make, and with more justice, for the aggregate exports to the continent were rising faster than those to the islands though the individual sugar-planter might consume more than any single North American. The planters, perhaps not very clear in the head themselves, confused the issue by arguing that they, unlike the northerners, repatriated their capital to England, which does not seem to have been true, for they were already beginning to fall deeper and deeper into debt to their factors at home.[2] They also said that, unlike the New Englanders, they improved the national balance of payments by furnishing a commodity for export.[3] By such means they appeared to have the better of the argument. Moreover, they had the stronger political influence; for, though the direct representation of absentee planters in parliament was probably overrated, they were beginning already, by intermarriage and education, to form social links with the governing class much stronger than those possessed by the continental colonies north of the Mason-Dixon line, which were their chief adversaries in the struggle. At any rate, right or wrong, the Molasses Act was passed.

The Act was passed, but not enforced. For a few years the more timorous merchants may have gone in fear of informers and confiscations, and instructed their captains to 'bring too down the river and send your cargo some to Road Island and

---

[1] Answer of the Island of Barbadoes to the Case for the Northern Colonies, December 1731, C.O. 28/22, Y. 115.

[2] [W. Cleland], *The Present State of the Sugar Plantations consider'd* (London, 1714), p. 25.

[3] This argument may have had some value in 1715, when re-exports of British sugar were still considerable; but it was almost worthless by 1733, when the re-export trade was reduced to a mere trickle, as the advocates for the Northern Colonies did not fail to point out.

some up here in boats, so as not to bring but a few hhds up to my wharf'.[1] The good people of Boston may perhaps have been sincere in January 1736 when they said that the Act had been 'the means of lessening the distillery of this town at least one half'.[2] But after the first splash was over, the Act proved to be a mere King Log dropped among the frogs. The duties collected and accounted for were small in the first few years, infinitesimal thereafter. Much of the foreign molasses was smuggled; but this can by no means have been universal, or there would be many more mentions of it in the merchants' correspondence. Probably more was disguised as British with the help of the corrupt and lazy Customs officials in the West Indies, who were ready to give certificates for imaginary quantities of produce which could be really taken on in the foreign colonies. Still more, perhaps, was entered in the North American ports, paying duties on a very small part of the cargo: 'Since you sailed from here', wrote Timothy Orne of Salem to George Dodge on 18 July 1758, 'our officers have recd orders not to enter foreign molasses as heretofore. The vessells that have arrived since those orders have been admitted to enter about one eighth or tenth part of their cargo paying 6d sterling p. gall. duty for what is entered—which is more than twice as much as was given before.'[3] Even so, it might have been worse.

After the Seven Years War, the Sugar Act and Grenville's attempt to enforce the regulations created a new panic like the first. The Browns of Providence were much concerned about the way the men-of-war might behave, and an officious Customs official, 'young Mumford', had to be reminded that 'he an't out of the reach of wants the favr of this town'.[4] Various kinds of clearances, ambiguous at least, were brought from the West Indies, some with success.[5] There was talk of

---

[1] James Browne to Captain Field, 6 March 1735/6, *Letter-Book of James Browne* (R.I.H.S., 1929), p. 21.

[2] Petition to the Governor and General Court, passed in Town Meeting of 1 January 1735/6, *Boston Records, 1729–1742, Boston Record Commission, Report no. 12*, p. 120.

[3] Timothy Orne MSS., iii, 136, Essex Institute.

[4] Nicholas Brown, Providence, to Moses Brown, Newport, 13 June 1764, Moses Brown Papers, i, 59, R.I.H.S.   [5] *Ibid.*

paying the fine, which would be cheaper than paying the
duties,[1] and the Browns thought for a moment (nor were they
alone in thinking) that it would be better to sell their vessels in
the West Indies than to face the trouble in the Custom-houses
at home.[2] This panic, however, was even shorter than the
other; it was relieved in 1766 by the Rockingham Ministry's
amended Sugar Act, which equalized the duties on British and
foreign molasses, thereby destroying the incentive to smuggle.

Even if the Act had been much better enforced than it was,
it probably would not have restrained the North Americans
from frequenting the French islands. They could not afford to
stop: as Obadiah Brown told his brother in 1738: 'if I stay hear
or at any of the Inglish islands I shall noot do that for you as
you sent me for: that is to gitt money'.[3]

Contact with the French was not always easy to achieve.
The French authorities were not always permitted to welcome
it, for the laws of France were against it and her merchant
interests thought themselves aggrieved by it—particularly the
exporters of flour, who made a much more serious attempt than
the English to keep their colonies supplied from Europe.[4] The
French merchants in the islands, however, were eager for the
North American cargoes, provided they could make their
market of them by preventing the captains from retailing them.
The planters usually contended that they could not live without these supplies. The Governors and Intendants were torn
between their duty and their common sense; their own interest
inclined them in favour of the latter, for they could exact heavy
fees from the North Americans for permission to trade. They
therefore took every excuse—almost permanently in war-time
and very often in times of peace—to open the ports of their
islands to a regulated trade.[5] Since, however, general freedom

[1] Nicholas Brown and Co., to A. Whipple, 13 January 1765, papers of Brig
George, Voyage 1764–5, Brown MSS., J.C.B.L.

[2] Orders to Capt. George Hopkins, 14 December 1764, papers of Ship *Nancy*,
ibid.; Timothy Orne to George Dodge, 18 July 1758, Timothy Orne MSS., iii,
136, Essex Institute.

[3] Obadiah Brown to James Browne, 5 March 1738, Moses Brown Papers, i, 5,
R.I.H.S.

[4] For the controversies on this subject, see my book, *War and Trade in the West
Indies*, pp. 343–90.

[5] *Ibid.*, pp. 352–9, 375–90.

was precarious and intermittent, the merchants and captains of North America (unless they were bold enough to chance their luck by entering the French ports with a feigned excuse or none at all) had to make sure of a reliable means of getting some kind of authorization.

There was more than one way of doing this. Many thought it safest to call at a British or neutral island and obtain some kind of introduction to the French. Thus Obadiah Brown went to St. Eustatius in the spring of 1738 and there got 'a very good lingester and one which is very well acquainted with the traid'; this, it seems, was 'Mr. Gooddel who is very well knone by all Rhoadisland men to be a very good man for such an afair'. He had good hopes of admittance at Martinique, for the capital had just been burnt down, and 'hear is nues of several vesels that have goot a permision for traid haveing horses and lumber on bord'. With this in view, Brown unloaded his tobacco in the road of St. Eustatius and bought lumber, in order to qualify himself for a permit.[1] This happy-go-lucky manner of proceeding may have been very well in such an emergency, but other people were more careful: for instance, the owners of the Schooner *Volant*, of Salem, instructed the master, Richard Derby, to call at Barbados and there, if he found the markets bad, to

> apply to Monsieur Monvielle or Nichols, for their terms in order to your going to Martinico or any other of the French islands, wch if they will answer accept of, they giveing us good & full security for your vessell & cargoe thear and whilest there and till your arrivall at Statia and not till then for their insurance to be void. . . . But before you absolutely engage with Monville, or Nicholls, . . . enquire of Mr. Clarke as to their credit and whither their interest among the French is so good as to be a protection for your vessell while there, and after you know what security they will give, then if you & Mr. Clark think you have propper security proceed according to their orders but not else.

A regular permit would have been much safer; and if Derby got himself admitted into Martinique in this somewhat irregular way, he was to 'secure a permitt so as for you to

[1] Obadiah Brown to James Browne, 5 March 1738, Moses Brown Papers, i, 5, R.I.H.S.

trade there the next voyage, wch you may undoubtedly do by your factor & a little greasing some others'.[1]

The Danish and Dutch islands were better places than the English for making arrangements of this sort: for it was there (especially to St. Eustatius when the Dutch were neutrals in war-time) that the French Governors sent down the permits to be disposed of. They also had other advantages, for they were free ports to which the planters and merchants of the neighbouring islands shipped goods on speculation. Much of the North American produce landed in the British Leeward Islands found its way to St. Eustatius and thence, no doubt, to the French: so much so, that when John Reynell complained to his factor in Antigua that another Philadelphia merchant's cargoes had been better sold, the factor replied, 'Mr. Meredith has alwise fitted his cargo's in the best wise for the newtrall & Dutch islands. . . . Your friend's factor has likewise got orders from gentlemen here on St. Eustatius for goods and money to a considerable value when going down in the sloop.'[2] Evidently the merchants of the British islands had effects there from the proceeds of such sales. St. Eustatius itself, and its open road, were a sort of exchange, or shop, where goods of all kinds could be bought, sold, or bartered without the trouble of long boat journeys with molasses or the risk of selling goods on credit to the dawdling planters or dunning them for produce in return. This is why a captain who was inactive or in a hurry would like to do business there: John Peck, one of the Browns' captains, hurt his leg and lost his ship's boat in a storm, so, as he wrote from St. Eustatius, 'we having no bot to assist ous and being very lame I thought it very improper to go to an English Island wheare both bot and activity was wanting. We steard along south till we made St. Martins and then this island.'[3] St. Eustatius had a further advantage: not only foreign West India produce but European goods too could be obtained there. The merchants of Rhode Island were, on the eve of the American Revolution, quite ready to import tea,

[1] Derby Family Papers, x, 2, Essex Institute.

[2] David Fogo to John Reynell, 27 January 1755, Coates-Reynell Papers, Box ix, H.S.P.

[3] John Peck to Nicholas Brown and Co., 25 January 1771, Brown MSS., J.C.B.L.

linseed oil, etc., by means of their whaling vessels which could touch at St. Eustatius in their cruises and bring home the forbidden or dutiable goods without suspicion.[1] The Danish islands were not nearly so useful, except when the Dutch were at war, which seldom happened after 1713. St. Thomas had once been the resort of pirates and smugglers, but St. Croix seldom had anything but its own produce to offer. According to a long letter in the Pemberton Papers, its trade was liable to arbitrary interference from Denmark, the masters of Danish ships might prevail upon the Governor to stop the North Americans from loading sugar until their own cargoes for Europe were complete, the court fees were exorbitant and 'such a shocking venality reigns thro' the whole that an Englishman cannot bear the thoughts of'.[2]

The Spaniards conceived the idea, during the Seven Years War, of setting up a free port at Monte Cristi on the northern coast of Hispaniola, a few miles from the French border. There was no harbour, no facilities of any kind, no real business men, and the whole place was a mere accommodation address for the French a few miles to leeward. It flourished greatly in the war, and was revived as a free port, with indifferent success, a few years after the peace.[3]

Best of all was to go directly to the French. Papers could be obtained in a number of ways. Sometimes a French merchant would arrive in the North American ports, equipped with what appeared to be valid papers, which he hawked round among the merchants in broken English.[4] A merchant in a French port might procure a permission and send it off to his correspondent in the hope that he possessed a vessel conformable to the description (it might give the purist French Customs officials a handle to make trouble if a snow or a brigantine arrived with papers which had been issued for a schooner or

---

[1] Aaron Lopez to John Turner and Son, 14 February 1765, Lopez Papers, Box i, Newport H[istorical] S[ociety]; Nicholas Brown and Co. to Mr. Jennings, St. Eustatius, 24 February 1774, Brown MSS., J.C.B.L.

[2] Charles Reade to James Pemberton, 16 December 1773, Pemberton Papers, xxv, 161, H.S.P.; 8 March 1774, *ibid.*, xxvi, 27.

[3] *War and Trade in the West Indies*, pp. 456–70.

[4] See the letter of 'R. M. Kingtown, or Villeroy', Boston, to Nicholas Brown, 18 July 1772, in Brown MSS., J.C.B.L.

a sloop).[1] Very often a North American who entered a French
port with no more than the hope of a permission would find
it quite easy to get one, if only he consented to grease the right
palms or put himself under the protection of a factor with the
right connexions. The permits were not always unconditional:
certain goods might be prescribed or barred, according to the
nature of the emergency which provided the excuse. Dry goods
were nearly always prohibited, except at the height of the
Seven Years War; flour was sometimes excluded if the ships
from France had lately arrived with a reasonable quantity.
Lumber, fish, horses and money were nearly always welcome,
and sometimes one of these was insisted upon as a condition of
the permit.[2] The conditions imposed by the French authorities
were subject to lightning changes. William Abbott thus
described the tergiversations after Guadeloupe was restored to
France in 1763:

> When the Ginnerall first arrived hear he gave permishion to all
> forren vesell to ankor and sell their cargo and load with rum and
> mollases and the 7 of this month he would not give promishon
> for fish but for lumber and rise pitch tar there wase no diffclty
> of any visell giting a pormishon for such artickles at that time
> but the 13th of this month the Ginnarall put up a procklamation
> that no vessell shall be admitted hear with any thing at present.
> But the Ginneral is as changable as the wind.[3]

Even if the authorities in the islands followed a consistent line,
something might go wrong. Strict orders to prohibit the trade
might arrive from Versailles, or a martinet might turn up in a
man-of-war: in September 1773 one of Aaron Lopez's captains
could do no business for six weeks at Cap François because of
'l'arrivée d'une frégate qui a fait surprendre les expedPositions

---

[1] See, for example, the letter of P. Rolland, Cap François, to Aaron Lopez,
7 April 1773, in Lopez Papers, iii, 64, Newport H.S.; Abraham Sarzedas to Aaron
Lopez, 22 April 1773, *ibid.*, p. 69.

[2] For example, at Martinique in the spring of 1738 (see Obadiah Brown's letter
quoted above, p. 59). See also *War and Trade in the West Indies*, p. 381. Horses
were always a *sine qua non* at Surinam.

[3] William Abbott to Timothy Orne and Co., 26 August 1763, Timothy Orne
MSS., xii, 38, Essex Institute; Israel Lovitt to Jonathan Gardner and Co., 20
January 1764, *ibid.*, xii, 60.

parce qu'elle visitoit et s'opposoit directement au genre de commerce que fait ici votre nation'.[1]

The French authorities were not the only ones who might take measures to spoil this trade. Though the Molasses Act was hardly executed at all before 1764, the British Government took very strong exception to intercourse with enemy colonies in time of war, and the British navy did much, though less than it might have done, to enforce the blockade of the French ports. The North American traders tried in vain to evade this blockade by means of 'flags of truce'—commissions from the Governors or judges in the British colonies authorizing them to visit the enemy colonies on the pretext of exchanging prisoners of war. I have described in another book[2] the embargoes, imposed by the local legislatures and even by Parliament, the seizures and the condemnations in the Prize Courts. These things undoubtedly cast a damp on the trade with the French. In the winter of 1757–8, when the blockade of the French colonies was only just beginning, Obadiah Brown was insuring voyages to the British sugar islands at 20 to 24 per cent, to the French islands at 15 per cent and even less (one flag of truce at 5 per cent). By 1761 most of the ships to or from the British West Indies were sailing at premiums of 10 or 12 per cent, while the North Americans trying to get home from Hispaniola had to pay 25 or 28 per cent.[3] Only the voyages to Surinam, still neutral and out of the way of hurricanes and privateers, remained as safe as ever;[4] and the traders to Monte Cristi, rightly confident that the Court of Prize Appeals would ultimately distinguish between them and the traders to the enemy, continued to operate at some relative advantage.

[1] P. Rolland to Aaron Lopez, 1 September 1773, Lopez Papers, iv, 18, Newport H.S.

[2] *War and Trade in the West Indies*, pp. 419–68.

[3] See the details of insurance policies in the Insurance Book of Obadiah Brown, R.I.H.S. The homeward voyage from the enemy colonies was much more dangerous than the outward voyage, because, as I have explained in *War and Trade in the West Indies*, pp. 442–6, it suited the men-of-war to let the North Americans into the French ports and catch them coming out.

[4] The insurance premiums to and from Surinam were the lowest of all in peace-time, and seldom rose above 12 or 14 per cent even in war-time. This was partly because there were said to be no hurricanes in Surinam. (See the letter of John Stamper and Co. to David Barclay and Son, 12 January 1753, Letter-Book of John Stamper, H.S.P.)

The economic effect of this trade is not easy to state. It must not be supposed that the forbidden markets were always better than the lawful. On the contrary, the papers of the Rhode Island merchants, for example, were full, especially in wartime, of complaints that the trade to the French colonies was overdone. Captain Thomas Rimington of the Schooner *Windmill* arrived at the port of Aux Cayes, on the south coast of St. Domingue, early in 1760, and found dry goods selling at 25 per cent loss and codfish at two pieces of eight the quintal. He soon found that he could not get even this price for his cod, and sold dry goods at 15 per cent loss. There were 28 other British vessels in the port, and molasses was got up from 10 pieces of eight the hogshead to 12 or 13, and likely to go to 15. He did not expect to get more than 80 hogsheads of it, and would probably have to wait two months for that.[1] He could hardly have done worse than this at Jamaica; indeed, a friend of his owners told them, a few months earlier, 'I am now about trying a voyage to our own islands (since trading with the enemy has turned out so very ill).'[2] Eleven years later another of the Champlins' captains had an experience of the same kind: at the free port of Cape Nicola Mole he found more than forty vessels to load with molasses, and not a hogshead in the harbour to be sold; the local traders took advantage of the scarcity to force the North Americans to take five or six hogsheads of bad sugar with every boatload of molasses.[3] Similar complaints went up from Monte Cristi, where, at the height of its vogue, the British and neutral vessels often numbered more than fifty, sometimes more than a hundred.[4]

Yet the trade went on; and, though many speculators must have lost money in the boom in flags of truce or in the rush to Monte Cristi, it is reasonable to suppose that it yielded a profit more often than not. Moreover, the markets at the British colonies would presumably have been far worse for the North Americans if they could not have gone to the French. The

[1] Thomas Rimington to Christopher Champlin and Co., 15 and 23 March 1760, Champlin Papers, unbound, Box 1732–1800, R.I.H.S.

[2] David Jamison, New York, to Christopher Champlin, 3 July 1760, printed in *Commerce of Rhode Island*, ed. Ford, i, 83.

[3] Thomas Rogers to C. and G. Champlin, 28 July 1771, printed, *ibid.*, i, 375.

[4] *War and Trade in the West Indies*, p. 457. The highest number was 130.

British sugar-planters said as much, and often tried to get the Molasses Act made more stringent or properly enforced. We cannot be sure that their outcries were always well founded, nor can we measure the difference that the trade to the foreign colonies made in the prices paid in the British. But presumably most merchants of North America would have agreed with Thomas Clifford of Philadelphia, who told his Barbadian friends in the autumn of 1759, 'We are in expectation of getting first cost for our produce in the West Indias this winter, as a great many merchants of this place as well as New York have turned trade into a new channel' . . . 'I really expect some trade to advantage this winter to our W. India islands though care seems always taken to supply Barbados well.'[1]

III. THE SALE OF THE OUTWARD CARGOES

When the cargo from America was assorted and the market in the West Indies at least provisionally chosen, the next thing was to determine how the goods should be sold. If the owner was not to go supercargo himself (which he very seldom did after 1700), he could entrust them either to the captain of the ship or to a factor living in the islands. The first of these alternatives was by no means excluded even if the vessel's destination was fixed; if not, it was almost inevitable, for hardly any North American merchant had such wide connexions as to possess a settled correspondent in every likely West Indian port.

Casual freighters of occasional parcels almost invariably consigned their little ventures to the captains; indeed, they may sometimes have had to do so, because they were using the cargo-space which constituted the captain's privilege.[2] A captain or supercargo who had the disposal of a number of small

---

[1] Thomas Clifford to Jonas Maynard, 15 November 1759, Clifford Correspondence, ii, 40, H.S.P.; to J. and T. Tipping, 16 November, 1759, *ibid.*, p. 42.

[2] In April 1769 Timothy Orne consigned ten boxes of soap to Joseph Lambert, master of the Brig *Ranger*, bound to Jamaica, allowing him the customary commission 'and then after takeing out the first cost as above, to allow the moiety or one half the remaining profit for the freight, the danger of seas excepted' (Timothy Orne MSS., vol. iii, Essex Institute). Clearly this must have been covered by the captain's privilege.

F

parcels might be tempted, in a fluctuating market, to treat some of his consignors better than others: it might be necessary to put him on his honour by some such phrase as this: 'I consign to thee notwithstanding I know thou has so much of the same goods (both thy own and others) knowing thou will do justly and hopeing I may be on equall terms with others for sales and dispatch.'[1]

The captains, of course, vaunted their own skill and probity in business, and even (it seems) tried to make their owners feel uncomfortable if they took any other measures for the sale of their goods. 'Our M^{rs}' (exclaimed Isaac Norris in 1709) 'by the extream generosity of some gent amongst us are become too toping for imploy, it is now call'd sneaking to consign a sloop to any but the M^{rs}'.[2] Yet not every ship-owner trusted his captains at their own valuation. James Browne of Providence even inquired behind the back of his own brother Obadiah about his sales in the islands.[3] No wonder if Obadiah felt his responsibilities rather heavy, and had to be reassured and admonished: 'Be sure to keep yourself in your right mind if possable, if any misfortunes attend you lay it not to heart, but consider that there is a higher power that governs all things, and if you are likely to meet with good fortune consider the same; and possibly these two thoughts may keep you in a medium as all men ought to be.'[4]

An owner might fetter his captain-consignee by giving him positive orders as to the choice of markets. This was not often done, for the chief advantage of consigning the cargo to the captain was the free choice of markets according to discretion and local circumstances. Yet it happened occasionally: in March 1763 the master of the Sloop *Polly* lamented that he could not sell his fish at St. Pierre, Martinique, where the market was excellent, because he was under positive orders to go to

[1] Isaac Norris to Edward Singleton, 18 December 1700, Isaac Norris Letter-Book, i, 255, H.S.P.

[2] Isaac Norris to George Mackenzie, 30 July 1709, *ibid.*, v, 48, H.S.P.

[3] This seems to be the meaning of his letters to Francis Rawls, 13 May 1736, and to Andrew Ardine, 21 May 1736, printed in *Letter-Book of James Browne* (R.I.H.S., 1929), pp. 29, 31.

[4] Instructions to Obadiah Brown, 10 February 1737/8, Moses Brown Papers, i, 4, R.I.H.S.

Barbados; strangely enough, in the next month Captain James
Ball wrote that he wished he could have sold in Barbados but
had been obliged to go to Martinique, where flour 'cannot be
lower unlest they give it away'.[1]

More often the captains had a virtually discretionary power
over their destination among the islands. Timothy Orne of
Salem and his partners habitually gave their captains conditional orders stuffed with ifs and an's, and more than once
concluded a page or two of hypothetical instructions by saying
'and in all cases & circumstances do that which you are well
assured will be best for us, as it is impossible for us to give you
particular directions how to act in all cases & circumstances,
we must and do leave the whole with you'.[2]

Captains armed with these discretionary powers sometimes
performed odysseys down the islands and back again, in search
of the best market. We hear of Richard Derby trying all the
islands from Montserrat to St. Eustatius, and of another captain
who went all the way from Antigua to Jamaica (but he seems
to have wanted not only a market but a freight to England).[3]
Many of these odysseys proved to have stopped in the wrong
place, as may be seen from the history of the captains in the
service of Thomas Clifford of Philadelphia.

In June 1756 Benjamin Canby wrote to explain how he came
to be selling his cargo at St. Kitts instead of Barbados: his sails
had been torn to pieces in a storm, he had lost his way in a fog
and made St. Kitts, whence he could not beat up to windward;
hearing that the markets were lower to leeward, he determined
to stay where he was. Six months later Jonathan Cowpland
also arrived at St. Kitts: he had been intended for Antigua but

[1] William Abbott to owners of Sloop *Polly*, 16 March 1763, Timothy Orne MSS.,
xii, 39, Essex Institute; James Ball to T. Fayerweather, 13 April 1763, Fayerweather MSS., N.E.H. and G.S.

[2] Instructions to Benjamin Bray, 18 September 1745, Timothy Orne MSS.,
i, 22, Essex Institute; to George Dodge, 11 September 1756, *ibid.*, iii, 34; to John
Hodges, 3 November. 1759, *ibid.*, x, 111; sailing orders to Simon Gross, n.d.,
Hancock MSS., Harvard University, Graduate School of Business Administration.

[3] Richard Derby, St. Eustatius, to Timothy Orne, 13 November 1743, Timothy
Orne MSS., x, 6, Essex Institute; J. Sherburne to J. Reynell, 6 July 1760, Coates-
Reynell Papers, Box xi, H.S.P.; see also the account of Captain Francis Board-
man's wanderings to Dominica, St. Vincent, St. Lucia, back to Dominica and then
on to St. Eustatius, June–September 1775, in MS. M. 656 1774, A. 2, Essex
Institute.

was chased into St. Kitts by a French privateer, and durst not
go further. Only a month later John Harper, who had been
intended for St. Kitts, turned up in Antigua for exactly the
same reason: he too had been chased by privateers, and saw,
after he had shaken them off, another strange sail between himself and St. Kitts. He therefore inquired of the markets at
Antigua before formally entering himself, found them bad but
did not know where else they would be better, so entered his
ship and cargo and then discovered that he could not get out
because of an embargo on the re-export of flour and a spell of
calm weather which, in his opinion, made the transit to St.
Kitts as dangerous as the whole voyage from Philadelphia to
Antigua. The next year Harper made a miscalculation: he was
lured from Antigua to St. Kitts by a report that rum was
cheaper; when he got there he found it dearer, and apparently
had to return to Antigua. Lastly, in 1763, this unlucky man
gave himself a lot of trouble for nothing. He touched first at
Antigua and St. Eustatius, where he found the markets for flour
bad, and learnt that they were still worse to windward, for
there was not an island where they would pay first cost and
charges. The only decent prospect he could hear of was at St.
Croix; but when he brought to outside the harbour and went
ashore, he discovered that the price of flour was only half what
he hoped. He resolved to go down to Jamaica rather than sell;
but a Danish man-of-war's boat brought his vessel by force into
the harbour, where he had to sell or pay the heavy port duties for
nothing. He could only console himself with the thought that
if he had sold at Antigua he must have waited two months for
his return cargo, and that in this universal glut (it was the first
season after a peace treaty) 'bad as this is I don't know where
I should have gone to done better'.[1]

These stories make it clear that most of the hindrances to
perfect mobility were of human contrivance. War always
weighted the arguments in favour of sitting down and selling
the cargo in the first port of call, both directly by adding to the

---

[1] Benjamin Canby to Thomas Clifford, 16 June 1756, Clifford Correspondence,
i, 155, H.S.P.; Jonathan Cowpland to Clifford and Pennington, 23 December
1756, *ibid.*, i, 195: John Harper to Clifford, 18 and 22 January 1757, *ibid.*, i, 207,
210; 16 February 1758, *ibid.*, ii, 34; 22 October 1763, *ibid.*, iv, 96.

danger of the seas, and indirectly by the embargoes on re-export which it provoked. A wary captain would try to find out whether any such restriction were in force, before committing himself irrevocably by entering his vessel: he would anchor outside the port, and go or send on shore for news; if the markets were bad or an embargo laid on, he would make for another port. (In order to defeat such precautions, the legislature of Antigua, having imposed an embargo in 1740, made the pilots swear not to reveal its existence to the masters of incoming vessels.[1])

Similar clogs upon free movement existed even in peacetime. Port charges varied from island to island, but they were mostly heavy enough, in proportion to the value of a small vessel's cargo, to make it advisable to sell the whole cargo at one place.[2] Some ports also imposed taxes on transient traders; these seem to have been levied on the whole value of the cargo: for example, the Kingston Vestry ordered in January 1781 that each transient person should be assessed on 'the first cost of his or their goods, wares or merchandize, or the amount of his or their invoice or invoices, cargoe and cargoes, which he or they may import, for sale, into this town or parish'.[3] The tax was sometimes remitted; the reason may have been that the captain only wished, or was able, to sell part of his cargo in the port. This, however, is not stated in the records: occasionally we find entries such as these: 'Constant Freeman. Assessed £24. Received £19 and gave him a receipt in full as he would pay no more', or 'Allen Kirkpatrick. His cargo being onions and not amounting to one hundred pounds would not pay it.'[4] The tax was hardly ever more than 2 per cent;[5] but it was

---

[1] *War and Trade in the West Indies*, p. 436.

[2] The port charges of the Sloop *Abraham and Jonah* at Antigua in 1731 are printed in *Commerce of Rhode Island*, ed. Ford, i, 21. They come to £14 11s. 9d. (strictly £13 11s. 9d., for a barrel of turpentine should not have been included). This would be something like 4 or 5 per cent of the average value of a sloop's cargo.

[3] Kingston Vestry Minutes, 17 January 1781, preserved in the Institute of Jamaica. Sometimes, however, the vestry imposed two different taxes, one on invoice values and the other on sales. If the taxpayer had the option between these, he need not pay on unsold cargo.

[4] Kingston Vestry Minutes, 5 March 1770.

[5] In February 1748/9 the transient tax at Kingston was fixed at only ½ per cent (Kingston Vestry Minutes). It had been higher during the war just ended. From 1770 to 1783 or later it was 2 per cent. The Kingston Vestry also discriminated

resented by the captains and supercargoes, perhaps because their owners expected them to pay it out of their own commissions.[1] More than once, at Bridgetown, Barbados, they tried to resist: on 12 July 1711 the Churchwarden of St. Michael's Parish 'laid before the Vestry an information he had received consisting of hard threats from several of the commanders of ships and other newcomers & non residents that they were resolved to make one common purse among them for opposing him in his duty of demanding & receiving from them the one pr cent on their trade assessed on them by the Vestry'.[2] The Vestry empowered him to fee counsel in his defence, and the opposition to the tax must have been dropped, for it was paid in later years.[3] Taxes of this sort may not have been unfair, but, if levied on the whole cargo, sold or unsold, they prevented the captains from moving freely from one market to another, and may even have discouraged the owners from consigning to the captains at all.

Most captains had as much latitude in the prices at which they might sell their cargo as in the places where they might carry it. The owners of a cargo of fish or flour might tell the captain not to take less than such and such a price for it with-

---

against transients by charging them higher rates than residents paid for burial fees and for the use of the parish funeral equipment. At Bridgetown, the capital of Barbados, it is hard to say certainly when the transient tax begins. On 9 July 1666 the 'merchants, traders, & artificers of this parish who are not freeholders of land & houses' were first separately assessed for parish taxation; in September 1675 certain persons are named (of whom one came from Piscataqua and one from Boston) as having paid sums of sugar for this purpose. Not until 7 March 1694/5 was a regular levy of 1 per cent laid upon 'the several masters of ships and merchants who shall a Rive'. This was not specifically repeated till 6 March 1704/5. The rate went up to 2 per cent in 1717, down to $1\frac{1}{2}$ per cent in 1729, and back to 2 per cent in 1732. This information is taken from Mr. Fitzpatrick's copies of the St. Michael's Vestry Minutes, which were kindly lent to me when I was in the island.

[1] Ezekiel Edwards, Barbados, to James Pemberton, 11 September 1772, Pemberton Papers, xxiv, 16, H.S.P.

[2] St. Michael's Vestry Minutes, 12 July 1711. There seem to have been further attempts at opposition in 1721 (Minute of 17 April 1721).

[3] From 1723 the sums paid are usually given. These figures give some idea of the transient trade in this port; but as they do not include cargoes consigned to resident merchants, and presumably do include cargoes of slaves consigned to the captains of slave traders from Africa, they give very little guidance as to the total value of the trade from North America.

out trying all the markets, and this was one cause for the peregrinations from island to island: thus it was reported from Barbados in June 1753 that 'there has some vessells gone past with their cargoes being consigned to the masters and the fish limited at 15s. p̄ quintal for the whole parcells, wch price nobody would give'.[1] But the owners of a mixed cargo would be ill advised to prescribe a minimum price for each article. The invoice prices of the goods were often stated in the captain's orders or in some documents annexed to them; but the owners usually went no further than to instruct him, as the Browns instructed their experienced Captain George Hopkins in 1764, to try to obtain these prices on an average for the cargo as a whole.[2] They did indeed fix a minimum price for the sales of their tobacco in Surinam and signed an agreement with the other exporters, stipulating that none of their captains should sell below that price during a stated period without consulting the others, nor lessen the price of his tobacco in order to get a better price for another article of his cargo.[3] But this was a part of a quite exceptional attempt at monopoly, which has already been described. Such combined attempts to obtain a fixed price were not unheard-of elsewhere, but they were unusual and probably most of them were unsuccessful.[4]

Having decided where to sell his cargo, a captain had next to choose between different methods of selling it. He might dispose of it as a whole; but this does not appear to have been usual. It happened sometimes at Jamaica, where the agents for a whole group of plantations, probably owned by absentees, were responsible for supplying a large and certain demand. These people, who also existed in Barbados under the name of 'town agents', were capable of contracting beforehand for

[1] Blackman and Adams to Timothy Orne and Co., 30 June 1753, Timothy Orne MSS., x, 44, Essex Institute.

[2] Orders to Capt. George Hopkins, 14 December 1764, papers of Ship *Nancy*, Brown MSS., J.C.B.L.

[3] Agreement of 18 October 1770, Brown MSS., *ibid*.

[4] David Fogo reported to John Reynell from Antigua on 15 February 1753 that the price of flour had been at 15/6 'but the whole of the flour that is on the island exclusive of what I have sold is not above 550 barrels and that is in the hands of transient traders who entered into combinations one with another the day before my arrivall to sell at 20/- which agreement I am entirely free from'. Evidently he meant to undersell them.

stores from North America, and even owned a few vessels in the trade; they were all that was left of the independent merchant class in the West Indies.[1] They were usually a separate class from the factors,[2] and for a very good reason: their customers, who understood very well that the goods they handled were their own property, kept them waiting months or even years for repayment, as one could not keep a factor waiting who had sold on commission and was being pressed for returns. For these reasons a town agent would excuse himself from accepting goods for sale on commission, and even a ship's captain who had made the same voyage several years running had to advise his owner, 'I really think it to our advantage to quitt this parrish for a year or two for this reason I am two well acquainted here they begin to demand credit much longer then I chuse to give them and if I refuse them they are much afronted and tell me, I may be damned and they will not deal with me any more.'[3] The town agents, however, bought whole cargoes, on occasion, from the captains and even made the task of the factors themselves easier: they bought larger parcels, and paid in cash; or, if they paid in produce, they gave at least as long a credit for what they sold as they received for what they bought. They therefore enabled the factors themselves to make quicker returns for their cargoes.[4]

The factors, properly speaking, themselves would sometimes 'take a cargo to themselves', that is, buy it on their own account at the market price. Perhaps it is no accident that we hear of this most frequently in the trade in New England fish, which, being perishable, had to be disposed of quickly. These

[1] *V. supra*, p. 9.

[2] Not quite always: Messrs. A. Sandiford and Son of Barbados, who were undoubtedly town agents, offered to sell cargoes of fish on commission (see their letter to Pemberton and Edwards, 16 November 1773, Pemberton Papers, xxv, 139, H.S.P.).

[3] Benjamin Wright to Aaron Lopez, 8 June 1770, Lopez MSS., Newport H.S.; *Commerce of Rhode Island*, ed. Ford, i, 174, 276.

[4] Birkett and Booth, Antigua, to John Reynell, 18 January 1752, Coates-Reynell Papers, Box iii, H.S.P. The merchant would not always want to buy the cargo whole; sometimes it would suit him better to buy from hand to mouth in the hope that cheaper supplies would arrive, and it would be the captain who would refuse to sell his goods in small parcels. (Esek Hopkins to the tobacco consignors, 7 January 1767, in papers of Sloop *Mary Ann*, Brown MSS., J.C.B.L.)

factors, on occasion, did more—they bought up other parcels
of fish in order to keep up the market, to the incidental advantage of their consignors, or they shipped some of their stocks to
other islands, for the same purpose.[1] The planters did not
always like to see the factors insert themselves in this way
between the captain and the consumer: in 1767 the Government of Surinam made an edict forbidding the 'English
marchants' to deal in horses, that the planters might buy them
straight from the ships.[2]

The merchants were not the captains' only customers. In
Barbados and Antigua we hear of 'hucksters', who dealt in
inferior provisions and fish oil.[3] Moreover, a captain could turn
retailer himself, and take a store. This was sometimes worth
doing for the sake of better prices, if the wholesale market was
so dull that sales would be slow in any case. But it did not
always answer, and some captains complained that they
suffered much by thefts.

A captain who acted as consignee of his cargo earned a commission, no matter how it was sold or to whom. The common
rate of commission was 5 per cent on sales and $2\frac{1}{2}$ per cent on
the goods purchased for the return cargo. The object of this
difference was obvious: to encourage the captain to sell his
outward cargo dear rather than buy West India produce dear.
Some owners accentuated it to the point of allowing $7\frac{1}{2}$ per cent
on sales and nothing on returns. Others again, for no assignable
reason, gave 5 per cent on each.

The hardest part of a captain's business was getting payment
for his cargo. One could hardly give a captain higher praise
than by saying that he was a clever and indefatigable collector
of debts.[4] Perhaps the North Americans did not have quite the
worst part of this business: different kinds of goods varied in
their power to command cash payment, and most articles of

[1] George Gascoigne and Sons, Barbados, to Timothy Orne and Co., 30
June, 14 July, 24 September 1753, Timothy Orne MSS., x, 44, 45, 62, Essex
Institute.

[2] Notification of 18 February 1767, Brown MSS., J.C.B.L.

[3] T. and J. R. Phillips, Barbados, to Timothy Orne, 24 April 1759, Timothy
Orne MSS., x, 125, Essex Institute.

[4] Captain Benjamin Wright is so described in the letter of Abraham Lopez,
Jamaica, to Aaron Lopez, 30 April 1767, Lopez MSS., Box i, Newport H.S.

North American produce, being both perishable and necessary, at least sold for quicker pay than dry goods.[1] Even so, it was laborious: captains quite often had to charge for horse hire in their accounts with their owners, and in some places, such as the out-parishes of Jamaica, the journeys were twenty or thirty miles long.[2] Where the business was done with merchants there might be less travel but just as much trouble of another kind: Silvanus Jencks, detained in Surinam by 'the bad pay of' the marchants', finally exclaimed, 'The villany of the marchants and most of the other inhabitants of this colony is grater than I can express by righting—which is the oneley reason of my being hear till this time.'[3] Some places had a worse name than others: Captain Benjamin Bray was thus instructed by his owners, 'We would caution you if you should go to Mounserat to be very carefull & cautious who you deal with for they are a people whom we would have you by no means to trust or confide in.'[4] But none was good.

Captains often excused themselves to their owners for taking something below the market price in order to get quick pay; but this could not always be done—if there was a glut of any particular article the term of payment for it was sure to be longer.[5] It was the commonest thing in the world to sell goods for payment in the next crop (February to June). In St. Croix many planters would only pay next crop but one.[6] Some captains would sell their cargo 'to be paid next vige', or would take a note of hand, which they would leave in the hands of a friendly merchant, instructing him how to invest and ship the proceeds

[1] Henry Bonnin of Antigua offered to return within two months the proceeds of bread and flour, 'but dry goods cannot so well answer, they not being saleable at all times' (Henry Bonnin to John Reynell, 2 April 1732, Coates-Reynell Papers, Box i, H.S.P.).

[2] A. P. Mendez, Jamaica, to Aaron Lopez, 11 March 1768, printed in *Commerce of Rhode Island*, ed. Ford, i, 231.

[3] Silvanus Jencks, Paramaribo, to Nicholas Brown and Co., 10 and 12 April 1773, Brown MSS., J.C.B.L.

[4] Instructions of 18 September 1745, Timothy Orne MSS., i, 22, Essex Institute.

[5] Joshua Howell, Barbados, to John Reynell, 1 October 1748, Coates-Reynell Papers, Box v, H.S.P.; David Fogo, Antigua, to John Reynell, 29 October 1753, *ibid.*, Box vii.

[6] Charles Reade, St. Croix, to James Pemberton, 8 March 1774, Pemberton Papers, xxvi, 27, H.S.P.

when they were received.[1] This was dangerous: George Hopkins explained to his owners that he did not expect to be able to sail with the convoy to Salt Tortuga 'without I leave the above goods heare and if I should God knows weather you ever would git any thing for them as I doant take them to be the best sort of people in the West Indias'.[2] Moreover, it was not only a question of honesty: those who left the proceeds of their cargoes to be shipped home in produce by another vessel, might be told that there was no freight to be had.[3] Some captains met these difficulties by entrusting to a fellow-captain the collection of any debts they might have to leave behind; this might also be a means of avoiding the payment of commission to a merchant for receiving the money—$2\frac{1}{2}$ per cent in most of the islands and 10 per cent in Surinam.[4]

Occasionally the need of overcoming this difficulty led to more elaborate schemes. 'If', wrote the owners to the master of the Schooner *Beaver*, 'you should be obliged to lay a considerable time for your pay, and can charter out our scooner to advantage we give you liberty for to do that.'[5] John van Cortlandt of New York had a brig which was intended to lead a double life: she carried a cargo to Nevis and left it for payment in the crop; she then returned to New York, carried another cargo to Barbados to be sold for immediate pay, and brought the proceeds of both cargoes home in one voyage. This was only possible because van Cortlandt, who owned a sugar-refinery, required his return cargo in the form of raw sugar, an expensive article in proportion to its bulk, which could easily represent the value of two outward cargoes.[6]

Schemes of this sort were all very well; but many ship-

[1] George Dodge to Timothy Orne and Co., 7 August 1757, Timothy Orne MSS., x, 90, Essex Institute; John Hodges to owners of Schooner *Beaver*, 9 January 1758, *ibid.*, xi, 63.

[2] George Hopkins, St. Eustatius, to Nicholas Brown and Co., 4 March 1765, papers of Ship *Nancy*, Brown MSS., J.C.B.L.

[3] George Dodge to Timothy Orne and Co., 4 July 1760, Timothy Orne MSS., xii, 12, Essex Institute.

[4] Nicholas Power, Paramaribo, to Nicholas Brown & Co., 29 June 1766, papers of Sloop *Four Brothers*, Brown MSS., J.C.B.L.

[5] Instructions to John Hodges, 9 November 1757, Timothy Orne MSS., iii, 69, Essex Institute.

[6] Instructions to Richard Mackey, 16 and 23 February 1767, John van Cortlandt Letter-Book 1762–1769, N.Y.P.L.

owners preferred, like Peter Faneuil, to instruct their captains, 'Be sure to see & gett every thing & leave nothing behind neither goods unsold nor return but bring all away with you.'[1]

A captain who could not by any means comply with this instruction might have to send home his vessel under the command of the mate and stay in the West Indies in order to sell the cargo and buy the returns.[2] The local merchants must have disliked the competition of these intruders; in Surinam they persuaded the Governor and Council to ordain that any master or supercargo who remained in the colony after his ship's departure must pay the same taxes and do the same militia duty as the inhabitants.[3] This may not have been altogether unjust. Some captains actually turned into resident factors— for example, David Fogo, one of John Reynell's captains, finally settled down as a factor in Antigua, doing some of Reynell's business in that capacity, and Darby Lux of Maryland graduated in the same way from the quarter-deck to the counting house.[4] Aaron Lopez's captains on the north side of Jamaica did not go quite so far as this, but, while continuing to command their ships for some of the voyages, they spent more and more of their time in the island and became so deeply rooted there as to take on some of the factor's character: for instance, they felt themselves obliged to provide and reserve for their regular customers a proper assortment of necessary goods, and their customers requited them by taking liberties in repayment which one could not take with a transient captain.[5]

[1] Instructions to John de Jersey, 31 July 1738, Peter Faneuil's Letter-Book, N.E.H. and G.S.

[2] For example, orders to Nicholas Power, 3 May 1765, papers of Sloop *Four Brothers*, Brown MSS., J.C.B.L.

[3] Annex to 'Notification' of 18 February 1767, in Brown. MSS., J.C.B.L.

[4] David Fogo asked John Reynell on 2 November 1754 to recommend him to any of his friends who wanted business done at Antigua, as it 'perhaps might inable me to settle here without going any more to sea' (Coates-Reynell Papers, Box viii, H.S.P.). William Lux went into the West India trade chiefly in order to consign the cargoes to his brother Darby, who, after a voyage or two as a transient supercargo, settled in Barbados as a factor and continued to receive William's consignments. (William Lux to John Bradford, 15 July 1768, Letter-Book of William Lux, N.Y.H.S.)

[5] Benjamin Wright to Aaron Lopez, 28 November 1768, Lopez Papers, iii, 22, Newport H.S.; 2 June 1769, 19 June 1773, printed in *Commerce of Rhode Island*, i, 276, 443; sailing orders to Captain Potter, 3 November 1769, *ibid.*, i, 296.

Another possible half-way house between captainship and factorship was a partnership between a captain and a factor. ✓ These were rare, but one was formed between John Harper, a captain in Thomas Clifford's service, and William Hartshorne of Antigua. 'Experience has taught me', Harper explained, 'that business is not to be done in the West Indies in the manner it was done formerly, that is it's impossible for the person that is mas^r of a vessel to sell a cargo otherwise than under the greatest disadvantages, he must either sell much under the value or detain the vessel so long in port that she sinks one half or more of her freight.'[1]

If captains could only sell their cargoes under such disadvantages, there was always an alternative—to consign the goods to a resident merchant, or at least to instruct the captain to put them into the hands of such a merchant if he could not sell them himself within a limited time. It is difficult to estimate how many owners chose this alternative. Certain great traders, such as Aaron Lopez and the Browns of Rhode Island, seem to have consigned nearly all their cargoes to their captains, except their ventures to the French islands where, as we shall see, special circumstances made a resident correspondent particularly necessary. So did Timothy Orne and Richard Derby of Salem. On the other hand the Philadelphia merchants—Isaac Norris, Jonathan Dickinson, John Reynell, Thomas Clifford and James Pemberton—seem to have done half their business, or more, through resident factors. Probably, taking the trade of North America as a whole, much less than half was done in this way.

The resident factor could point to certain advantages which he possessed over the transient supercargo. For one thing, since cash prices were normally much lower than credit prices, he could turn out for the owners a much better account of sales than their captain could, by selling at longer credit.[2] He might, of course, complain that he was hindered from doing so by the competition of the transient traders themselves, who

---

[1] John Harper to Thomas Clifford, 27 January 1765, Clifford Correspondence, iv, 145, H.S.P.

[2] George Gascoigne and Co., Barbados, to Timothy Orne and Co., 30 June 1753, Timothy Orne MSS., x, 44, Essex Institute.

sold at absurdly low rates in fear of each other. The factors'
letters to North America are full of lamentations upon this
subject, and of calculations as to the number of different hands
among whom the stocks at market were currently held—
eleven was considered a large number in the flour trade at
Antigua.[1]

A factor in good standing might also be expected to advance
all or part of the return cargo before the outward cargo was
sold. How he obtained the capital to do this, we do not often
know. We hear of a factor who had 'the advantage of a
London credit' and could therefore draw for £200 or £300 at a
time in order to advance West India produce for his Philadelphia correspondent, but there is no knowing how common
this was.[2] With or without such advantages, many factors
rendered this service, or, at least, were asked to render it.
Timothy Orne told his captains that if they had to leave part
of their cargoes in the hands of the merchants of Barbados, they
should obtain as large an advance as they could, and this they
sometimes succeeded in doing.[3] Philip Cuyler expected a
quarter of the value of his outward cargo to be advanced; and
John van Cortlandt imagined an ideal scheme for his brig to

---

[1] Same to same, 30 August 1753, *ibid.*, x, 45; Birkett and Booth to John Reynell,
15 September 1747, Coates-Reynell Papers, Box v, H.S.P.; David Fogo to John
Reynell, 11 February 1752, 15 February 1753, *ibid.*, Box vii. Even the captains
themselves often complained of each other for selling in too great a hurry: see
Joshua Howell's letter to John Reynell, 3 September 1748, *ibid.*, Box v, and Benjamin Wright's outburst: 'They are such damn'd miserable puppies that useth
this port, they are frightened to death if people do not appear to purchase their
cargoes immediately, and should nobody appear to purchase, they then fall the
price immediately, I was selling superfine flour at 35/-, then came in two vessells
from Philadelphia they landed their flour directly, and asked no more than 30/-
for the superfine flour, which has obliged me to sell at the same price, or keep my
flour on board' (Benjamin Wright to Aaron Lopez, 8 November 1768, Lopez
MSS., iii, 22, Newport H.S.).

[2] David Fogo to John Reynell, 27 January 1755, Coates-Reynell Papers, Box
ix, H.S.P. Messrs. Lascelles and Maxwell of London appear from their papers to
have made very extensive advances for their friends who had merchant houses in
Barbados. These advances were chiefly, though not all, connected with consignments of slaves or with victualling contracts. Some British merchants, such
as the Pinneys, disliked advancing money for merchants in the islands, who could
not give landed security like the planters. (See my book, *A West India Fortune*
(London, 1950), pp. 240–3.)

[3] Instructions to Benjamin Herbert, 18 March 1750/1, Timothy Orne MSS., i,
114, Essex Institute; to Benjamin Bates, 30 May 1750, *ibid.*

make five voyages a year by inducing his factor to be always the
value of one return cargo in advance.[1] Some owners were
willing to allow a consideration for these advances;[2] but
interest does not seem to have been charged very often. It
seems to have been held usually that a consignor was entitled
to obtain dispatch in this way from the merchant upon whom
he conferred the favour of the consignment and the commissions to be drawn from it.[3] Some merchants formally
offered a preference to any factor who would advance so much
or invest on his own account in the return cargo; but such offers
were not always accepted, for not many people in the islands
had money to invest in this way.[4] There was, in every case,
a limit to the credit which the factors could give, even if they
had the necessary money and were willing to forgo, in the
interest of their correspondents, the opportunity of using it on
their own account.[5] 'It was not in our power', wrote Messrs.
Birkett and Booth of Antigua to John Reynell,

> to advance so largely for the two cargo's you've consigned to us,
> owing to the extream bad complyances we meet with last year
> from those indebted to us, we are as willing as any people to
> oblige our friends in that or any other shape, but you're sensible,
> that if payments are not made to us, it is totally out of our power
> doing it . . . here our planters gives no credit for their produce,
> but frequently has a part of the money advanced 'em before the
> goods agreed for are delivered.

A few months later they wrote again,

> You may depend on our assiduity in the collecting the debts due
> on yours & our other friends' acco[s], and that no delay shall be
> given in the remitting of them, but our crop producing very

[1] Philip Cuyler to Thomas Durham, 20 February 1760, Letter-Book of Philip
Cuyler, N.Y.P.L.; John van Cortlandt to Alexander Stephenson, 10 February
1766, John van Cortlandt Letter-Book, 1762–1769, N.Y.P.L.

[2] Isaac Norris to Richard Poor, 5 April 1700, Isaac Norris Letter-Book, i, 161,
H.S.P.

[3] Isaac Norris to Abel Bond, 6 July 1703, *ibid.*, ii, 66.

[4] David Fogo to John Reynell, 14 January 1754, Coates-Reynell Papers, Box
viii, H.S.P. (Although David Fogo declined to comply with Reynell's proposal, he
afterwards thought better of it, and raised £130 for the purpose.)

[5] See the quotation from Thomas Kerby's letter, printed by Mr. Byron Fairchild
in *Messrs. William Pepperrell, Merchants at Piscataqua*, pp. 54–5.

short this year, the planters could not discharge their acco[s], and it is in their hands that most of our money lays, judgeing it the more secure than in other of the inhabitants.[1]

This letter, and many others, make it clear that the factors sold most of the cargoes under their care to the planters, though not to them alone, for the hucksters and town agents, where such persons existed, were also their customers. The goods were sold in large lots or in small: two accounts of sales which John Reynell's factors rendered of his flour show that it was sold in parcels of 1 to 60 and of 1 to 109 barrels.[2] Sometimes they advertised it in the local papers at his expense, and sold it by auction; but this was usually regarded as a counsel of despair.[3]

There was some dispute as to the factor's obligation to make good bad debts. Most factors seem to have disputed it, and to have considered that if they were so incompetent or so unlucky as to sell their correspondent's goods to bad customers, his proper remedy against them was to withdraw his business from them.[4] A consignor could induce his factor to guarantee him against bad debts in return for a special allowance; the rate was not generally fixed, but when Dr. Dicker of Exeter tried to make his correspondent in Antigua do it for 2 per cent, the correspondent complained that he was being 'tied to hard meat'.[5]

These were the main services that a factor could do for his correspondent in North America; but there was one class of special cases where something more was necessary. Admission to the French islands could often be obtained only by a special permit; and the authorities often doled out these permits to their own friends among the merchants or, at least, only granted applications made through some merchant or other. This put the merchants in a strong position, and they made a

---

[1] Birkett and Booth to John Reynell, 18 January and 14 June 1752, Coates-Reynell Papers, Box vii, H.S.P.

[2] Accounts of sales for 1751, *ibid.*, Box vi, H.S.P.; accounts of sales, 23 September 1752, *ibid.*, Box vii.

[3] Accounts of sales, 26 May 1753, *ibid.*, Box vii.

[4] W. Sandiford, Barbados, to James Pemberton, 7 September 1774, Pemberton Papers, xxvi, 147, H.S.P.

[5] Henry Bonnin, Antigua, to John Reynell, 3 April 1732, Coates-Reynell Papers, Box i, H.S.P.

charge for their help and favour—according to one captain, 10 per cent on the value of the outward cargo was the rule at Guadeloupe in 1763.[1] They would also, of course, expect the consignment of the cargo, which would bring them in a further commission. Even the somewhat dubious characters who wandered round the British colonies, claiming that they had the power to get a vessel admitted at French ports, would make demands of the same kind. Some of these people were frauds. Captain Bradford of the Browns' Sloop "A" had great trouble with one Peter Begeris, with whom he was to share his commissions in return for the necessary introductions. 'As to Peter,' he wrote, 'I dont no but he may be onest & he is as ignorant as he is onast, for he can due no sort of bizness at all and as for the jentelmun that he said was his frind and wold give him the prefernce of his molases all the frind ship he showes to him is he tells me that he wonders how any body will trust him to sell or bye any thing for he is fit for nothing but a common sailer.'[2] The simple North American captains were often mystified by the way the French merchants ran each other down;[3] but they had to make the best of it, for they could not do without them even when they were allowed the legal right to deal with the planters directly. 'All though there was no objection to my doing my one business,' wrote Samuel Haynes from Fort Dauphin in 1763, 'yet after trying a few days I found theere was sum duficulty in it as wee are obliged to barter the greatest part of the cargo to the planters for their produce, & I being a stranger did not know who I might safely trust & who not: therefore to avoid such difulty I agreed with Mr. Langlea [?Langlois] to give him a comition on the cargo.'[4]

For all the services he thus performed, the factor was requited by a commission. The usual rates were 5 per cent on sales and 5 per cent on returns, and $2\frac{1}{2}$ per cent for paying or

[1] Jacob Crowninshield, St. Pierre, Martinique, to owners of Brig *Betsey*, 7 October 1763, Timothy Orne MSS., xii, 44, Essex Institute.

[2] William Bradford, 'Lamanard', to Nicholas Brown and Co., 3 February 1773, papers of Sloop "A", Brown MSS., J.C.B.L.

[3] 'French men sildom or ever spakes well of one another for sum pepel ses one thing and sum another' (John Archer to Richard Derby, Derby Family Papers, vol. xii, Essex Institute).

[4] Samuel Haynes to Thomas Fayerweather, 4 August 1763, Fayerweather MSS., N.E.H. and G.S.

G

receiving money that was not directly connected with the sales of goods. These were higher rates than those of the captains; but the factors had not, like the captains, any privilege cargoes.[1] They thought themselves underpaid, and tried, not without success, to raise the rates towards the end of the period. 'I had rather do business in Phil[a] for 2½ p̄ ct', wrote W. Smith of Barbados to Thomas Clifford in 1770, 'than here for 12½'; and again: 'You cannot have any idea of the fatigue & trouble of selling & collecting in this island or I'm sure you'd hardly think 12½ p̄ Ct. too much, if its worth 10 p̄ Ct in Phil[a] it certainly must be worth more in this expensive part of the world— indeed many times you'd say trade will not bear more but it was a few years past 15 p̄ Ct for sales and returns.'[2]

It is hard to state generally what kind of income these commissions yielded to the factors. Some of them became great men, like John Reynell's correspondent Samuel Dicker, who returned from Jamaica to England with a fortune large enough to enable him to sit in parliament. Probably this fortune did not all come directly from the factor's business though that might be its ultimate origin; for the successful in every other walk of life turned planters. Perhaps the short and humble career of William Lloyd is more representative. He arrived at St. Anns, on the north side of Jamaica, to take up a partnership with a Mr. Osborne, who had connexions with New Hampshire and claimed to have made £1,000 a year in the trade. The first year's business was not promising: only £600 was earned in commissions, from which £200 had to be deducted for storage and negro hire. William Lloyd's share of the remainder was one-third, which only exceeded his expenses by £6 7s. 4d. Soon afterwards he set up for himself, and in the year 1751 he made £897 10s. od. from which £383 10s. od. was deducted for storage and other expenses. Of the balance he invested £197 17s. 6d. in beds and furniture for his store, also apparel. A little later he entered into another partnership with a Mr. Temple, who was to have seven-twelfths of the profits as he brought with him much business from New Hampshire, though

---

[1] *V. supra*, pp. 21–3.
[2] W. Smith to Thomas Clifford, 4 and 18 November 1770, Clifford Correspondence, v, 175, 178, H.S.P.

Lloyd himself had a brother who consigned some vessels from Boston and New York. On 27 November 1754 William Lloyd died of a fever brought on by over-exercise. He certainly had not made a fortune.[1]

No doubt there were good, bad and indifferent factors, and it is only natural that we should hear most about the bad. They were certainly much complained against, especially for their unjustifiable delays in returning the proceeds of cargoes committed to their hands.[2] A few of them absconded, or became bankrupt for spectacular sums—Gedney Clarke the younger of Barbados, it was said, for £100,000 to £150,000 in 1774.[3] Captains and supercargoes from the puritan colonies of the north could not condone their unbusinesslike habits, which seemed to border on dishonesty. Ezekiel Edwards, a prig fresh from Philadelphia, thus condemned the merchants of Barbados:

> A person cannot be too cautious how he connects himself with a Barbados merch^t, for many of them keep no books & if they can procure money enough to furnish their tables every day with barbecued fish & sangree, they are entirely regardless how their acco^{t}s run on—& most of them will bear dunning for years together without any marks of shame, & perhaps promise ten times a day if you can meet them so often, that they will pay in an hour. It is a very good place to sell a cargo, but if a stranger don't take care it will be to persons who never intend to pay him.[4]

Thus the clerk from Philadelphia; a Rhode Island captain expressed the matter, as one might expect, a little more forcibly when he exclaimed against the merchants of Surinam, 'I bleve thair is more honner and honesty in so many highwaymen in England then in the marchants of this place.'[5]

The consignees of cargoes, whether they were transient

[1] *The Lloyds of Lloyds Neck, Long Island* (*N.Y.H.S. Collections*), i, 421–2, 479, 484, 490, 495, 527.

[2] See, for example, the letter from Samuel Sewall's apprentice to Nathaniel Barnes of Antigua, 8 March 1689–90, *Letter-Books of Samuel Sewall* (*Mass. H.S. Collections*), i, 108.

[3] John Hawksworth, Barbados, to James Pemberton, 30 May 1774, Pemberton Papers, xxvi, 75, H.S.P.

[4] Ezekiel Edwards to James Pemberton, 17 October 1772, *ibid.*, xxiv, 44.

[5] Esek Hopkins to Nicholas Brown and Co., 22 March 1767, papers of Sloop *Four Brothers*, Brown MSS., J.C.B.L.

captains or resident factors, needed all their skill to sell their
goods to advantage in the very difficult markets of the West
Indies. Only three ports—Bridgetown in Barbados, Kingston
in Jamaica,[1] and above all the Dutch island of St. Eustatius,[2]
were markets of conspicuous size or wide commercial connexions. The capitals of the lesser islands were glutted by a
very few cargoes—still more so the smaller towns like Spikes-
town, Barbados.[3] Lumber was the only article of American
produce which could be stored for several months; this was
often necessary as the demand was concentrated in crop-time.[4]
Nearly everything else was more or less perishable: not even
flour kept long in the tropics;[5] fish was notoriously perishable,
though fish packed in hogsheads had some advantage over fish
in bulk, and a merchant could hold the former for a short time
rather than sell in a market swamped by supplies of the latter;[6]
oil leaked, unless it was quickly put into jars, and some captains

---

[1] The merchants of Kingston, both before and after the establishment of the
South Sea Company, did a great deal of business, especially in flour, with the
settlements on the Spanish Main. The state of this trade was often reported to
affect the Kingston market for flour and other North American produce. (Isaac
Norris to J. Pinnell, 29 July 1699, Letter-Books of Isaac Norris, i, 35, H.S.P.;
Samuel Bean to John Reynell, 14 April 1756, Coates-Reynell Papers, Box ix,
H.S.P.)

[2] St. Eustatius was, in a sense, the commercial metropolis of the neighbouring
British and French islands: many small craft brought produce to its road and the
best news of markets was to be had there. For these reasons many owners instructed
their captains to touch first at St. Eustatius for news (cf. Thomas Hancock's sailing
orders to Captain Simon Gross of the *Charming Lydia*, n.d., Hancock MSS.,
Harvard University Graduate School of Business Administration).

[3] 'Spikesis is such a small place sune gluted' (John Lovett to Timothy Orne,
23 January 1745/6, Timothy Orne MSS., x, 14, Essex Institute).

[4] John Reynell appears to have instructed his factors in Antigua to keep his
lumber till next crop unless they could sell it at £10 the thousand. (Birkett and
Booth to J.R., 5 January 1752, Coates-Reynell Papers, Box vii, H.S.P.) Not all
supercargoes had enough sang-froid for this, especially when they knew that more
lumber was on its way to market. (Ezekiel Edwards to James Pemberton, 17
October 1772, Pemberton Papers, xxiv, 44, H.S.P.) The planters, for their part,
mostly bought lumber from hand to mouth, that is to say, in crop-time. Only an
intelligent man like John Pinney would buy in the off-season when the North
American captains were anxious to wind up their sales and get away.

[5] James Child, Kingston, to John Reynell, 25 August 1764, Coates-Reynell
Papers, Box xii, H.S.P. Musty flour would not be a total loss, so long as it was
good enough to feed the slaves. (Birkett and Booth to John Reynell, 15 August
1747, *ibid.*, Box iv.)

[6] T. J. and R. Phillips, Barbados, to Timothy Orne, 27 November 1757,
Timothy Orne MSS., x, 91, Essex Institute.

with oil in barrel found themselves at a disadvantage because they could not get hold of any jars. (Probably many planters, who bought oil from hand to mouth and especially in crop-time, were themselves no better off for storage; when some people at the west end of Jamaica bought oil in the off-season and stored it for themselves, Captain Benjamin Wright was so much taken aback by the avowal of this unusual practice that he described it as 'impudent'.[1]) It did not take large quantities of these perishable goods to produce what the merchants considered as a hopeless glut: sometimes the quantities reported to have had this effect were surprisingly small.[2]

The competition which produced these results sprang from many quarters. Sometimes it was the straightforward competition of specialists from the same port selling the same article: for instance, when we learn that in the chief port of St. Lucia, on 31 July 1769, twelve Newburyport captains celebrated the good news of their Governor's recall by inviting the Salem captains and other gentlemen to a very fine entertainment, including a barbecued hog, we cannot help reflecting that there must have been a great deal of fish for the market of so small an island.[3]

It was for the purpose of enabling their consignees to deal with this competition that owners so often sent them information of recent or impending departures; unfortunately this information often proved misleading, chiefly because the length of the voyages was unpredictable, so that one vessel was quite likely to start before another and arrive after her.[4] Even if the

---

[1] The same to the same, 24 April 1759, *ibid.*, xi, 125; Benjamin Wright, Savanna-la-Mar, to Aaron Lopez, 28 November 1768, Lopez MSS., iii, 22, Newport H.S.

[2] For example, 600 hogsheads of fish in store were enough to glut the market of Basseterre, the capital of Guadeloupe, so that 'times neaver were worse' (Samuel Herrick to Timothy Orne and Co., 29 July 1762, Timothy Orne MSS., xii, 26, Essex Institute). 5,000 barrels of flour, even 2,500 or 2,000, was regarded as a very large supply at Antigua, but 500 or 600 was spoken of as a small one.

[3] Log of Schooner *Sally*, M. Hodges commander, MS. M. 656, 1768 D, Essex Institute.

[4] Timothy Orne and Co. to Adams and Blackman, 18 December 1751, Timothy Orne MSS., vi, 76, Essex Institute; for an example of the danger of relying on this kind of information, see Messrs. Gascoigne's letter of 30 August 1753 to Timothy Orne, *ibid.*, x, 45. Similar information about the impending return voyages from the West Indies was useful to the merchants at home: the Browns of Rhode Island

departures from a single colony could have been calculated reliably, far too little was known about the other colonies; and since certain articles—flour, pork, and, above all, lumber— might arrive in the West Indies from a number of different places, the chance of disappointment in the markets was great.[1] The disturbances were sudden and revolutionary—only too often the consignees reported that a week had made all the difference.[2] Competition from other colonies was not the only danger; Europe itself continued to compete in certain branches of business. Ireland exported large quantities of beef and pork to the West Indies; it was cheaper and better than the North American article.[3] Both England and France sent some flour to the West Indies. It was, indeed, one of the few provisions which the merchants of France, especially those of Bordeaux, made some effort to send out to the colonies even in war-time; and the arrival, or even the expectation, of a convoy from France was enough to depress the market.[4] Flour occasionally arrived in the islands even from England. This had been quite common in the seventeenth century. Isaac Norris wrote in 1710 as if supplies of flour from Europe were now unnecessary: 'altho' corn has been dear in Europe yett the N. America has so increased in it and over-stockt the plantations in

---

instructed Captain Whipple 'by all means in every letter you write mention how many Eng^sh vesels in port, the masters names, & where they belong & how much mel^s each wants of there load with a gen^l price cur^t.' (Instruction of 9 October 1764, papers of Brig *George*, Brown MSS., J.C.B.L.) Some of their captains diligently complied with this instruction.

[1] Captain T. Gilbert of Philadelphia had to sell his lumber very cheap at Antigua in January 1751, because he found the island glutted with lumber from New England and New York (see his letter to John Reynell 15 January 1750–1, Coates-Reynell Papers, Box vi, H.S.P.).

[2] *Ibid.* Three days was enough to reduce the price of bread at St. Kitts from 50/- to 30/- and that of flour from 36/- to 25/-. (Timothy Sheehan to Thomas Wharton, 12 August 1760, Wharton Papers, Box vi, H.S.P.)

[3] Isaac Norris to Job Williams, 1 August 1699, Letter-Books of Isaac Norris, i, 38, H.S.P.

[4] On 21 July 1746 Nathaniel Palmer reported to Timothy Orne that the convoy from France had brought nothing but flour and wine (Timothy Orne MSS., x, 20, Essex Institute). The first fleet from France after the Seven Years War reduced the price of all American provisions in occupied Martinique (Samuel Herrick to Timothy Orne and Co., 22 May 1763, Timothy Orne MSS., xii, 36; James Ball to T. Fayerweather, 26 April 1763, Thomas Fayerweather Commercial Papers, N.E.H. and G.S.).

the West Indies that wee have sold to excessive loss last year'.[1] But Jonathan Dickinson reported, nearly ten years later, without any strong accent of surprise, that there were no buyers for flour in Philadelphia, 'having acco^t from Barbadoes that a great quant^y of London flower about a thousand cask in one week wch occationed that commodity to sink to 7s 6d p̄ Cwt.'[2] By the middle of the century supplies from this source seem to have been no more than occasional: Messrs. Birkett and Booth of Antigua prognosticated in February 1751 that 'if the harvest in England last year was anything like plentifull we imagine that the vessells from thence will come out provided with bread; it will be much if the Londoners does not also bring out some also for sale'.[3]

Lastly, the flour and Indian corn of North America competed with the ground provisions—yams, potatoes, and even plantains—which the planters grew for the Negroes' diet or the Negroes grew for themselves. It was the official theory, especially in war-time, that every plantation ought to be able to feed itself and that provisions from North America should only be a supplement for an emergency. Hardly any plantations ever lived up to this theory; but they grew enough to make the ground provision harvest a bad season for selling flour in Antigua and a drought or a hurricane a bull point for flour.[4]

The fluctuations of the market were, of course, much aggravated by the vagaries of weather and politics. The Philadelphia traders 'galloping away to avoid the frost' at the end of December might create a temporary glut in the islands, but a long, hard winter in North America, which reduced sailings even below what was normal for the season, would enable the

[1] I.N. to Joseph Pike, 18 February 1709–10, Letter-Books of Isaac Norris, v, 134, H.S.P.

[2] J.D. to Lewis Galdy, 1 June 1719, Letter-Book of Jonathan Dickinson, p. 248, L.C.P.

[3] Birkett and Booth to John Reynell, 12 February 1752, Coates-Reynell Papers, Box vii, H.S.P.

[4] Isaac Norris to J. Pinnell, 12 June 1699, Letter-Books of Isaac Norris, i, 5, H.S.P.; Birkett and Booth to John Reynell, 12 February 1752, Coates-Reynell Papers, Box vii, H.S.P.; Bayly, Elworthy and Bayly, Jamaica, to John Reynell, 13 April 1754, *ibid.*, Box viii, Thomas Tipping, Barbados, to Thomas Clifford, 26 September 1757, Clifford Correspondence, ii, 8, H.S.P.

factors in the West Indies to clear off their stocks.[1] A hurricane nearly always created a great demand for lumber by blowing the roofs off the buildings, and for flour by destroying the plantains and the ground provisions;[2] it might even improve the markets next year, for the reminder it administered was apt to deter some North American traders from allowing their vessels to lie in the islands in the next hurricane season, so that those who dared to stay would have the field to themselves.[3] The effect of war was equally obvious. An embargo in North America was like a frost: it enabled the merchants in the islands to liquidate their stocks or caused them to congratulate themselves upon having kept goods by them;[4] an embargo in the islands produced the contrary result, by preventing the merchants from relieving their superabundance by re-export to another market.[5] The arrival of a great fleet from Europe was sure to create a demand for some provisions, and at any time during a war the demand of the agent victualler and even of the privateers was a thing to be reckoned with.[6] If one of these expeditions should lead to a conquest, it might open a valuable new market: the prices of provisions were maintained, at the beginning of 1759, by the hope that Martinique or Guadeloupe would be conquered and, indeed, the capture of Guadeloupe did create a lively trade, though only for a time.[7] On the other hand, admirals were regarded in certain quarters as spoil-sports: there are many references to the disagreeable effect of

---

[1] John Watts to Gedney Clarke, 2 January 1762, *Letter-Book of John Watts* (*N.Y.H.S. Collections*, lxi), p. 8; Birkett and Booth to John Reynell, 3 April 1752, Coates-Reynell Papers, Box vii, H.S.P.

[2] Same to same, 14 September 1751, *ibid.*, Box vi (but it appears from their letter of 4 October 1751, *ibid.*, that this hurricane did not affect the market so much as they expected); same to same, 24 September 1752, *ibid.*, Box vii.

[3] Same to same, 14 June 1752, *ibid.*

[4] John Reynell to David Fogo, 24 May 1756, Reynell Letter-Book i, H.S.P.; John Watkins, St. Kitts, to Thomas Clifford, 22 September 1757, Clifford Correspondence, i, 291, H.S.P.; Thomas Tipping, Barbados, to Thomas Clifford, 26 September 1767, *ibid.*, ii, 8.

[5] John Harper, Antigua, to Thomas Clifford, 18 January 1757, *ibid.*, i, 208.

[6] Daniel Flexney and Rodrigo Pacheco to John Reynell, 12 August 1740, Coates-Reynell Papers, Box ii, H.S.P.; Birkett and Booth, Antigua, to John Reynell, 15 August 1747, *ibid.*, Box iv; John Watkins, St. Kitts, to Thomas Clifford, 9 March 1757, Clifford Correspondence, i, 222, H.S.P.

[7] Thomas Wharton, St. Kitts, to Thomas Wharton, Philadelphia, 2 January and 24 July 1759, Wharton Papers, Box ii, H.S.P.

Commodore Moore's paper blockade upon the trade of St. Eustatius.[1] Sales were often interfered with by the competition of prize goods, for the captors, who had come by their cargoes without paying for them, usually sold without any regard for the state of the market; the impact of prize goods upon the markets would be all the greater because privateering would already have withdrawn shipping from normal trade, so that normal supplies would be lower.[2] Moreover, war interfered generally with the free movement of goods from one British island or port to another; and this clearly was the chief means by which not only transient traders but resident factors too protected themselves against low prices—there are many references, for example, to shipments of flour or other North American produce between the islands of the Leeward group or between Kingston and the outports of Jamaica.[3]

The correspondence of merchants contains so much more complaint than congratulation that one might well suppose bad luck to have been commoner than good in the West India markets. It was, however, a very unfortunate consignee, or one with a highly specialized cargo, who had bad luck with every single article. Usually some goods turned out well, if others did badly. This fact is visible in such records of turn-out as we have. For example, the invoice and sale prices of the cargo of the Browns' Sloop "A", from Providence to 'Lemena' or 'Lamanard' in Hispaniola, December 1772–February 1773, compare as shown on the following page.

It will be seen that the lumber was much the most successful part of this cargo, the butter the worst; some of the fish turned out considerably better than others, the hogs' fat twice as well

---

[1] John Harper, Antigua, to Thomas Clifford, 19 December 1757, Clifford Correspondence, ii, 20, H.S.P.; George Dodge to Timothy Orne, 14 December 1757, Timothy Orne MSS., x, 86, Essex Institute; George Dodge, St. Eustatius, to Timothy Orne and Co., 27 March 1759, *ibid.*, xi, 78. For an earlier alarm of the same kind at St. Eustatius, see the letter of Nathaniel Palmer to Timothy Orne, 3 January 1745/6, *ibid.*, x, 14.

[2] Fitch Pool, St. Eustatius, to Timothy Orne, 15 September 1758, *ibid.*, x, 99.

[3] Birkett and Booth, Antigua, to John Reynell, 16 October 1747, 23 January 1753, Coates-Reynell Papers, Boxes iv and vii, H.S.P.; Benjamin Wright, Savanna-la-Mar, to Aaron Lopez, 28 November 1768, Lopez Papers, iii, 22, Newport H.S.; Benjamin Allen, St. Anns, Jamaica, to Aaron Lopez, 12 August 1771, *ibid.*, iii, 39.

as the tallow. From what we know of this voyage, none of the
perishable goods seem to have suffered by excessive delays; the
prices appear to have reflected fairly the state of the market,
which was generally bad—the master reported that 'There is
nothing but flower and candles but what is cheaper here then
at Rhod Island.'[1]

	Invoice Price (Lawful Money, Rhode Island)	Sale Price (St. Domingue currency)
7½ barrels pork, per barrel	72/-	96 livres
10 barrels beef, per barrel	48/-	42
3,000 hoops, per thousand	54/-	150
6 hhds. codfish, per cwt.	14/-	15
44 barrels menhaden, per barrel	12/6	16 livres 10 sous[2]
12 barrels alewives, per barrel	16/6	17
25 bars iron, per cwt.	27/-	27
18,000 long staves, per thousand	72/-	180
10 half-barrels pork, per ½-barrel	40/-	36-40
4 ditto beef, per ½-barrel	26/-	18-24
8 firkins butter, per lb.	8d.	3 sous
15 cwt. cheese, per lb.	5d.	12-15 sous
10 kegs hogs fat, per lb.	6d.	1 livre
16 kegs tallow, per lb.	6d.	9 sous

If the owners of such mixed cargoes sometimes gained on the
swings what they lost on the roundabouts, this was not in every
case the result of blind chance. Sometimes one article would be
sold below the market price in order to get a better price for
another, or to sell it at all: thus one of the Browns' captains
sold some tobacco low in order to get inferior horses off his
hands, and Benjamin Wright told his employer 'am under no
apprehension, but shall be able to get 2/6 for our cargo of
candles, have had them at 2/9 p̄ pound, find it will not do am
sensible it will prejudice me in selling my other cargo providing
I hold they candles so high'.[3] When the ship herself was for

[1] Papers of Sloop "A", 1772, Brown MSS., J.C.B.L. The Brown MSS. are
unusually rich in the materials for comparisons of this sort, but the example I have
chosen is, I think, the completest and most intelligible.

[2] 20 sous equal 1 livre.

[3] Abraham Whipple, Surinam, 8 November 1764, papers of Brig *George*, 1764–5,
ibid. (In 1770 the Browns agreed to forbid practices of this sort; such an under-
taking was a necessary part of the cartel for the export of tobacco to Surinam—for
which, *v. supra*, pp. 45, 71—since it stopped a loophole for concealed competition in
price-cutting between the members.) Benjamin Wright to Aaron Lopez, 28
Novembre 1768, Lopez Papers, iii, 22, Newport H.S.

sale, her price and that of the cargo might affect each other: at one time a cargo would sell better with the vessel than without, at another time the boot would be on the other leg.[1]

[1] Richard Derby and Co., to Mevrow Godet, St. Eustatius, 21 December 1745, Timothy Orne MSS., i, 19, Essex Institute; George Dodge, St. Eustatius, to Timothy Orne and Co., 18 February 1757, *ibid.*, xi, 58.

CHAPTER III

THE RETURN CARGOES

I. THE PURCHASE OF RETURN CARGOES

THE sales of northern goods in the islands cannot be considered apart from the purchase of the return cargoes. The two operations were inseparable in the merchants' minds, though it was only in the earliest days that they formed part of the same transaction, either by a contract of barter or by the sale of goods for a price reckoned in West India produce as currency. (Even then, such currency could be exchanged into other kinds of goods, as when John Huntley rendered an account of sales at Barbados in which refuse fish was disposed of at 1 lb. tobacco per lb. fish, the tobacco being afterwards exchanged for cotton at 2 lb. tobacco per lb. cotton.[1]) In later times, even though produce had been superseded by other money of account, the merchants looked to the profit of the whole voyage, as measured by the relation of the value of the returns to that of the outward cargo and the ship's outgoings; and their captains, when deciding whether to sell at current prices, kept in mind the current valuation of the produce which they expected to buy.

The choice of return cargo varied according to a number of different circumstances. In the first place, it had to depend on what was available; and the several islands varied somewhat in their characteristic produce. This applied particularly to the two great West Indian exports to North America—rum and molasses. Rum, of course, was distilled from molasses; but in some islands the planters normally had stills, in others they had not. It was the older and better developed colonies (like Barbados and Antigua) that usually sold their molasses distilled into rum; the newer (such as Jamaica, at first, and St. Kitts, which had to be settled or resettled after the Peace of Utrecht)

[1] *Aspinwall Notarial Records*, p. 140 (1 July 1648).

that let the North Americans have their molasses raw. This fact comes out clearly in the figures: in 1726–30 the average exports from Barbados and the Leeward Islands to North America are as follows:

	Sugar lb.	Rum gallons	Molasses gallons
Barbados	685,682	680,269	54,378
Antigua	263,758	235,966	25,256
Nevis	77,882	25	181,249
St. Kitts	197,017	4,399	121,173
Montserrat	29,950	9,711	14,781

The figures for Jamaica are not exactly comparable, being expressed in casks of various sizes; but they give the strong impression of an enormous preponderance of molasses over rum.[1] This impression is confirmed by most of our other information. Round about 1700 Barbados was much the largest exporter of rum to New York.[2] It is significant that molasses is only mentioned once or twice in twenty or thirty years of John Reynell's correspondence with Antigua, though that might be explained another way: rum was not only the chief produce of Antigua but also the article most in demand at Philadelphia. So much did the merchants of that town depend on Antigua for rum that they somewhat preferred the island to others as a market for their own goods: Robert Ellis, in 1738, left the master of the *Sarah and Elizabeth* free to sell at St. Kitts if the market was much better, 'But rather yould dispose of it at Antigua for you'l be more likely to get rum there.'[3]

The choice of a return cargo was also, of course, determined by the requirements of the market at home. I have already mentioned, for example, the fact that rum bore quite a high proportion to molasses in the imports of Philadelphia—a much

[1] *Calendar of State Papers, America and West Indies, 1732*, no. 98. These figures are not very reliable: those for Barbados and the Leeward Islands are derived from the collection of the 4½ per cent export duty, and are probably under-estimates; in Jamaica there was no reason for collecting reliable figures at all. But in neither case was there any motive for falsifying the proportion of rum to molasses.

[2] Almost exactly half the rum imported into New York between 1 January 1700/1 and 31 July 1703 came from Barbados (New York, Hall of Records, Old Conveyances, Lib. 30).

[3] R.E. to Seth Drummond, 8 July 1738, Letter-Book of Robert Ellis, p. 107, H.S.P.

higher proportion than in those of Boston. In 1769 Boston imported, from the West Indies, 1,190,754 gallons of molasses and only 71,937 gallons of rum, whereas Philadelphia took only 352,855 gallons of molasses and 734,342 gallons of rum. In 1771 the contrast was much the same: Boston took from the West Indies 1,096,496 gallons of molasses and 57,305 gallons of rum, Philadelphia took 435,176 gallons of molasses and 521,085 gallons of rum.[1] This contrast is confirmed by some earlier figures;[2] no doubt it is to be explained by the much greater strength of the distillery industry in New England, to which I have referred already.[3]

Besides these local tastes or circumstances which affected the demand for rum or molasses at a particular place, there were general limitations upon the demand for the other West Indian staples. Isaac Norris of Philadelphia remarked in 1703 that a very little of the minor crops—ginger, indigo or pimento—was enough to glut the market.[4] Even sugar, though an article of

[1] Massachusetts Historical Society, MS. 026.4 (Accounts of goods imported into North America).

[2] In the year 25 March 1730–25 March 1731, according to the *American Weekly Mercury* (6 May 1731) the net imports (after deduction for re-exports) of rum into the port of Philadelphia were 1,369 hogsheads, 1,156 tierces, 39 barrels; of molasses, 236 hhd, 1,550 trs., 22 barrels. In the year 25 March 1734–25 March 1735 (*ibid.*, 27 March 1735), the corresponding figures for rum were 1,530 hhd., 489 trs., 18 barrels; for molasses, 1,083 hhd., 13 trs., 19 barrels. In Boston, on the other hand, the figures of 'West India goods imported at the Impost Office' are as follows:

	Sugar			Molasses			Rum		
	Hhds.	Trs.	Barr.	Hhds.	Trs.	Barr.	Hhds.	Trs.	Barr.
April–April									
1755—1765	373	46	736	4,236	148	68	665	6	8
1756—1757	538	836	699	4,493	141	109	340	40	9
1757—1758	579	190	236	3,838	88	10	1,344	39	18
1759—1760	1,087	312	284	4,852	361	23	1,021	59	9
Jan. – April									
1762—1763	718	336	457	3,434	2,244	28	371	69	–

(Of these figures, which are presumably of gross imports, the first four come from the Lowell Papers in the Massachusetts Historical Society, the last from the papers of the Society for encouraging Trade and Commerce, MS. 91 L, in the same Society's Collection. These last give the provenance, showing that in 1762 three-quarters of the sugar and nearly 95 per cent of the molasses, but hardly any of the rum, came from the French sugar islands then occupied by the British.)

[3] *V. supra*, pp. 29–34.

[4] I.N. to William Watson, 17 June 1703, Letter-Books of Isaac Norris, ii, 59, H.S.P.

much commoner use, did not meet with an unlimited sale in
North America: Jonathan Dickinson, likewise of Philadelphia,
advised a correspondent not to send the finer sorts, since the
coarser were preferred,[1] and very probably the use of sugar
among the poorer classes in North America was limited by the
competition of its own cheaper by-product, molasses—for it is
difficult to believe that the floods of molasses that entered the
North American ports were all distilled into rum, insatiable
though the demand for rum might be. The figures I have
already quoted[2] show that the volume of sugar imported into
Boston was comparatively small (though the value was pro-
portionately higher), and it is significant that some Salem ship-
owners prescribed to their captains, as a general rule, to ship
one-third of the value of an outward cargo in sugar, two-
thirds in rum.[3]

The choice of a return cargo also varied, of course, according
to the prices of the several sorts of goods in the islands, and their
relation to the probable market prices at home. This relation
could not be calculated very exactly; the latter of its two terms
often fluctuated in a manner which took the merchants by
surprise, and, since communication with the islands was only
intermittent, the latest developments could not always be
known there. Sometimes, however, enough was known of them
to convince a particular captain that he had better not buy a
given article.[4] At other times the merchant, presuming on
what he knew of the current price and the probable seasonal
variations at home, would set down for his captain's guidance
the prices beyond which it would be inadvisable to go in the

---

[1] J.D. to Isaac Gale, 7 September 1717, Letter-Book of Jonathan Dickinson,
p. 142, L.C.P.

[2] See p. 94, note 2.

[3] e.g. Timothy Orne to Joseph Grafton, 28 December 1757, Timothy Orne
MSS., iii, 73, Essex Institute. On this occasion there could be no question of
adjusting the proportions between the various kinds of goods in a return cargo
so as to produce exactly a full loading (a practice which I shall describe below)
for the goods were to be shipped home in another bottom; so we may suppose
that one-third of the value in sugar to two-thirds in rum was considered the
proper ratio for imports into Salem from Barbados.

[4] A captain wrote to his owners from St. Eustatius in May 1761 that, having
just heard from a new arrival that molasses was 'very logh at home', he had altered
the ship's voyage (George Dodge to Timothy Orne, 16 May 1761, Timothy Orne
MSS., vi, 16, Essex Institute).

islands.[1] This was all very well; but the captain's freedom of
choice was only limited, since he had to buy something after all.
To return in ballast was to confess failure, and to ruin the
owner.[2] To obtain a freight homeward would not be so bad;
but, though some owners permitted their captains to do this,[3]
goods on freight were not always to be had and were most
likely to offer when rum and molasses were plentiful and cheap
in the islands—just the circumstances when the captain could
do without a freight. Unless, therefore, an alternative use
could be found for the ship in the islands, such as a freight to
Europe or a salt voyage,[4] the captain or the factor must buy
some kind of produce, whether it was likely to answer or no.

He had to deal with variations and discrepancies of prices
which might arise from a number of causes. The supply of
sugar, rum and molasses fluctuated (usually in close correlation
with each other) according to the success of the crop, which was
at the mercy of the weather and, sometimes, of war emergencies. These fluctuations were particularly wild at Antigua,
which depended on a very capricious rainfall: 'this year's crop',
reported Nathaniel Booth of that island in August 1754, 'has been
a miserable one indeed, not above three thousand hhds. of sugar
made, and of course but little rum, whereas last year there was
exported 22 m. hhds. of sugar and abundance of rum made'.[5]

---

[1] This must be what Jonathan Dickinson meant when he wrote, 'if rum is
above 18d ℘ gall. will not yeild here above 2/- therefore the less may do' (J.D. to
John Lewis, Jamaica, 31 May 1716, Letter-Book of Jonathan Dickinson, p. 76,
L.C.P.). Richard Derby twice set down, for his captains' guidance, the 'prices of
such goods as will answer at this market'. These prices he expressed in Massachusetts currency, leaving the captains to translate them into the currency of the
island where they did business (Orders to Captain Henry Elkins, 23 January
1764, and to Captain David Ropes, 19 June 1766, Derby Family MSS., vol. xxvii,
Essex Institute).

[2] Nevertheless, we hear of 'Captain Humphrey Clase who returns in his ballast
as rum is above your limits & much too high for any markett abroad' (Birkett
and Booth, Antigua, to John Reynell, 18 January 1752, Coates-Reynell Papers,
Box vii, H.S.P.).

[3] Instructions to William English, 9 June 1712, printed in *Essex Institute Historical
Collections*, i, 168; Thomas Clifford to Samuel Smith, 4 August 1761, Clifford
Correspondence, vol. xxvii, H.S.P.

[4] Both these things will be referred to more fully below—the salt voyages on
pp. 103–4 and freights for England on pp. 154–6.

[5] Nathaniel Booth to John Reynell, 10 August 1754, Coates-Reynell Papers,
Box viii, H.S.P.

But the islands did not all have the same weather: one might have a short crop when another had a full one, and the price of produce might be raised or lowered at one island by the knowledge of the bad or good prospects of another.[1] So far as the North American captains had freedom of movement between one island and another, and chose to exercise it, they might even the prices of produce among the islands by refusing to pay too much at one place and resorting to another. Some of them did so, or spoke of doing so.[2] But they could only do this if they could get their outward cargoes paid for in cash. They managed it sometimes, but not very often: hard cash was perennially scarce in most of the British colonies, few planters would pay their debts in anything but produce, and therefore few merchants commanded anything but produce.[3] A captain must usually be ready to buy his return cargo where he sold his outward cargo: most of them wrote as if this were an understood thing, and it was one of the considerations which they and their owners had in mind when they fixed upon a market.

The prices of the West Indian staples might be said to vary, at any rate in the short run, according to the supply and the demand, the supply being the more uncertain of the two. But the demand which governed the market was not only that of the North Americans themselves. The price of sugar in the islands was ruled by its prospects in the London market: so much so that, down to the end of the seventeenth century, sugar, though still accepted as a currency, was a currency

[1] 'There is a very discourageing acco^t from Barbados concerning their crop which with the hurricane that was at Jamaica we fear will occasion rum and sugar to break high at this markett' (Birkett and Booth, Antigua, to John Reynell, 5 January 1752, *ibid.*, Box vii).

[2] 'When thou comest to Bb^{dos} before thou proceeds further consider as well how sugars or other returns may be held as well as how provisions will sell and also consider that thou may sell for 2 or 3 s. in a cwt lese at Bb^{ds} then at Neves or Antigua yett if thou sell there and carry afterwards the money down to Antigua or Nevis it advances 20 p̄ ct saves 30 s. a tunn, and the other charges etc. and is generally the quicker markett' (Isaac Norris to Richard Phillips, 25 July 1699, Letter-Books of Isaac Norris, i, 35, H.S.P.). John Reynell's correspondents in Antigua several times advised him to let his captains leave the island and take their cash to St. Kitts for rum, or advised him that other captains had done so (David Fogo to J.R., 11 February 1752 and 27 April 1753, Coates-Reynell Papers, Box vii, H.S.P.).

[3] John Martin, Antigua, to John Reynell, 18 September 1755, *ibid.*, Box ix.

H

whose valuation was reckoned upon the net proceeds per hundredweight in London.[1] Rum, too, seems to have been affected by the English demand. This is more surprising, for most of the rum was sold to the North Americans: more than 90 per cent in Barbados and Antigua at the end of the seventeenth century, and apparently 100 per cent in some of the other islands.[2] Only the rum of Jamaica acquired any real reputation in England, and that not much before the middle of the eighteenth century. Yet the planters, even in the colonies whose rum was esteemed inferior, must have been aware of the London market as a possible stand-by or speculation: Messrs. Lascelles and Maxwell, for example, sometimes thought it worth while to quote the price of rum to their correspondents in Barbados and the Leeward Islands, and occasionally disposed of a parcel for them. Therefore the expectation of a convoy for

[1] See my book, *A West India Fortune* (London, 1950), pp. 34–5.

[2] The figures given for Barbados, 1687–1706, in a manuscript formerly in the Chalmers Collection and now in the Library of Congress ('Papers Relating to Barbados, 1663–1762') are as follows:

		25 Dec. 1687 to do 1689	13 Feb. 1691 to do 1692	25 Dec. 1697 to do 1698	25 Dec. 1698 to do 1699	25 Dec. 1699 to do 1700	25 Dec. 1704 to do 1705	25 Dec. 1705 to do 1706
To England:								
Sugar:	Butts	112	1,306					
	Hhds.	1,414	12,862	25,970	15,881	21,815	16,537	17,963
	Tierces	54	1,144	1,858	1,144	1,428	1,540	2,101
	Barrels	206	1,849	7,075	3,376	4,242	3,064	2,917
	Casks	48	2,824		4	158		
	lb.			8,800				
Rum:	Hhds.	276					30	
	Tierces	36	Nil	1	4	Nil	5	
	Barrels	19					24	1
Ships		14	70	117	90	115	74	71
To Plantations:								
Sugar:	Butts							
	Hhds.	124	309	97	128	177	83	65
	Tierces	33	107	64	67	58	26	28
	Barrels	415	323	1,622	910	2,201	1,715	1,482
	Casks	56	577		286	94		
	lb.	278,528	398,249					
Rum:	Hhds.	1,109	1,599	2,264	1,704	2,907	2,896	2,872
	Tierces	366	1,402	2,284	1,693	2,426	1,818	1,789
	Barrels	1,462	2,388	2,549	1,629	2,749	1,799	1,723
	Casks	29	89	859	1,811	782		
Ships		88	116	141	153	182	113	117

England sometimes affected the price of rum at Barbados or Antigua;[1] still more in Jamaica, where the price was more obviously governed by the news from England.[2] Occasionally a vessel in ballast from Scotland or one with beef from Ireland would take in rum at one of the smaller islands, making it scarcer and dearer than the North Americans liked.[3] Of the products of the sugar-cane, only molasses was relatively un-influenced by the English demand, for it was hardly ever exported to Europe; and even molasses might feel the pull of the English market indirectly wherever the planters possessed stills which would enable them to turn their molasses into rum if they judged it profitable; which was the state of affairs almost all over Jamaica by the middle of the eighteenth century, at Barbados and Antigua at a much earlier date, and though uncommon, was by no means unknown at the other British sugar islands. Only at a comparatively backward French or Dutch colony like Surinam or Guadeloupe, with no more than a local demand for rum, do we find that the planters could do nothing with their molasses but sell it to the North Americans; and it can hardly be an accident that these are the colonies where we hear most about the North Americans combining in order to keep the price down.[4]

When captains, supercargoes or factors had to choose between these West India products, one of the chief considera-tions (besides price and profit, the most important of all) which governed their choice was the desire to ship the proceeds of the outward cargo in a full return cargo, neither more nor less. It is easy to see the disadvantage of buying a larger return cargo than the vessel could carry: it was unwise to leave effects

---

[1] Edward Dowers, Antigua, to John Reynell, 27 August 1746, Coates-Reynell Papers, Box iv, H.S.P.; E. Winslow and Co., Barbados, to Timothy Orne, 17 August 1747, Timothy Orne MSS., x, 24, Essex Institute. It is just possible that these reports of the demand created by the impending departure of a convoy refer to the consumption of the crews of the convoy itself; for any large collection of seamen heightened the demand for rum wherever they were. But I think that is the less natural interpretation.

[2] Benjamin Wright, Savanna-la-Mar, to Aaron Lopez and Co., 2 January 1768, printed in *The Commerce of Rhode Island*, ed. Ford, i, 217.

[3] David Fogo, Antigua, to John Reynell, 27 April 1753, Coates-Reynell Papers, Box vii, H.S.P.

[4] For these attempts, *v. infra*, pp. 105–6 and 119.

behind in the hands of the dilatory and untrustworthy West Indians and, at the very least, they could only be got home at the cost of outgoings, which no frugal merchant liked, for freight on another merchant's ship. (When a ship-owner had two or more vessels plying to the same West Indian port, as Aaron Lopez had in Jamaica and the Browns at Surinam, combinations of this sort favoured economy and timing without outlay, and were highly advantageous.) It is hardly less easy to see why the return cargo ought not to fall short of the vessel's capacity: besides the Yankee or Quaker dislike of wasting anything, even space, it happened that molasses, the article which usually yielded most profit,[1] was also the bulkiest, so there was a strong inducement to fill the vessel up. This inducement was not counteracted by the consideration that the freight and cooperage of molasses were just as expensive as those of the more valuable rum, for most importers of molasses had it carried in their own vessels, and sent their own coopers to set up the cask, so as to avoid out-of-pocket expenses. The owners, therefore, often exhorted their captains to 'proportion your loading back with as much molasses & the remainder in sugar so as to load the vessell on account of the owners'.[2] They recognized, however, that their agents might not always be able to follow this counsel of perfection: one captain had liberty to take goods on freight if the proceeds of his outward cargo would not quite buy a full load home,[3] another to ship home the surplus on another vessel if the proceeds of his outward cargo would buy too much.[4] Occasionally the disproportion was more marked: the Browns of Providence, whose outward cargoes (containing horses, cattle and spermaceti candles) were rather valuable, more than once expressed the hope that one outward cargo would buy two return cargoes of

[1] Esek Hopkins to Nicholas Brown and Co., 14 January 1767, papers of Sloop *Mary Ann*, Brown MSS., J.C.B.L.

[2] Christopher Champlin, instructions to Captain Thomas Rimington, 15 December 1759, Champlin Papers, Box 1732–1800, R.I.H.S.; there is a similar phrase in the instructions of Captain William Bradford of the Sloop "A", 14 December 1772, Brown MSS., J.C.B.L.

[3] Instructions to William English, 9 June 1712, printed in *Essex Institute Historical Collections*, i, 168.

[4] Timothy Orne and Co., to William Webster, 20 February 1754, Timothy Orne MSS., ii, 90, Essex Institute.

molasses,[1] whereas John van Cortlandt, who, being a sugar-refiner, wanted his returns in sugar, expected two outward cargoes to buy one return cargo.[2]

If the captains had been limited to ringing the changes on sugar, molasses, and rum, with occasional resort to freight or ballast, the task of adjusting the returns to the outward cargo would have been difficult, for some islands offered very little rum, others very little molasses, and there was a limit to the amount of sugar that could profitably be taken. But fortunately there were other means of escape from this dilemma. One of them consisted of the so-called 'light pay'—the minor West Indian products whose value was high in proportion to their bulk. One or more of these might enable a captain with a cargo of molasses to adjust his equation at the last moment, or, when molasses was scarce or dear, to mitigate the disgrace and loss of a voyage home in ballast. The most important of these minor crops were cotton, cocoa, indigo and coffee. There was not a large demand for any of them in North America, though some of the New England colonies had encouraged the importation of cotton in the early days when it was needed to quilt clothing as a protection against the arrows of Red Indians.[3] There was a further limitation to their use in a return cargo: cotton was the only one of them to be found almost everywhere, the others were only produced at Jamaica or the French islands, though they could also be had at St. Eustatius and Curaçao, those two Dutch islets which served as general emporia for everything that was bought or sold in the Caribbean. (This was, no doubt, one of the reasons why so many North Americans frequented them: the problem of composing a return cargo was easily solved there.)

There were other ways of dealing with the difficulty. A captain returning from the West Indies could find other things to bring with him besides West India produce. Some owners were not averse from having part of their effects invested in

---

[1] Nicholas Brown and Co., to Nicholas Power, 30 April 1767, papers of Brigantine *Sally*, 1767, Brown MSS., J.C.B.L.; to Captain S. Smith, 4 September 1770, papers of Brig *Sally*, 1770, *ibid.*

[2] *V. supra*, p. 75.

[3] See the orders of 8 February 1640 and 4 October 1642, *Connecticut Public Records*, i, 59, and *New Haven Colonial Records*, i, 214.

Negro slaves, who were to be had in the West Indies, whether creoles or raw Africans.[1] Others were ready to take part of their cargoes in European goods. This was quite common in the early days, before the northern ports began to specialize in commercial activity and the West India islands in tropical agriculture: thus we hear of dimity sent from Barbados to Boston in 1659 as a better return than sugar, and Isaac Norris of Philadelphia (still a young colony in 1700) sometimes instructed his correspondents to ship his returns in holland or cambric, though at other times he doubted whether European goods would answer.[2] In the same period European goods sometimes reached North America through the West Indies in a rather peculiar way. It was the great age of piracy, and goods spoiled by pirates were freely bought and sold at Jamaica.[3] All these things became unusual by 1750, but there were still some European, though not British, goods which it paid to bring from the West Indies: such, for example, was sailcloth, which could be had not only from St. Eustatius but from a quite uncommercial Dutch colony like Surinam.[4]

On rare occasions the northern captains brought home cash from the West Indies. This seems to have been common in the seventeenth century but to have virtually ceased in the eighteenth; for both Governor Cornbury in 1708 and Cadwallader Colden in 1723 wrote as if the Dutch colonies and, occasionally, Jamaica were now the only places from which money was imported into New York.[5] Even Jamaica could not be relied upon, though it abounded in cash when the trade to the Spanish colonies flourished under cover of the South Sea Company's activities: for Jonathan Dickinson, though eager for ready

[1] Robert Ellis, Philadelphia, to David Hall, 22 April and 22 November 1740, Letter-Book of Robert Ellis, pp. 197, 253, H.S.P.; William Lux, Baltimore, to Darby Lux, Barbados, 27 February 1764, Letter-Book of William Lux, N.Y.H.S.

[2] John Hulott, Barbados, to George Little, Newbury, Mass., 17 May 1659, printed in *New England Historical and Genealogical Register*, xlv, 282–3; Isaac Norris to Richard Poor, 6 July 1699, Letter-Books of Isaac Norris, i, 21, H.S.P.; to Jonathan Dickinson, January or February 1699/1700, *ibid.*, i, 135.

[3] John Style, Jamaica, to Sir W. Morice, 14 January 1688/9, Public Record Office, C.O. 1/24, no. 8.

[4] Instructions to Captain Abraham Whipple, 16 September 1764, papers of Brig *George*, 1764–5, Brown MSS., J.C.B.L.

[5] Lord Cornbury to the Board of Trade, 1 July 1708, *N.Y. Col. Doc.*, v, 57; Colden's account of the trade of New York, 1723, *ibid.*, v, 685.

money, wrote in 1717 that no money came from Jamaica but light coin, which would not do.[1] Dickinson, like other people, had to resort to the French colonies for cash. The authorities of those colonies were more likely to insist on the North Americans importing cash than to let them export it. Sometimes they winked at the exportation; but even then, some North Americans thought it a confession of failure to take cash rather than a commodity which would have yielded a profit.[2]

It was more to the purpose to take the use of cash in the West Indies without the cash itself, by borrowing money on the owner's credit in order to buy produce. Debts of this sort could be discharged by drawing a bill of exchange on the owner, if only anybody could be found to accept such a bill. That does not seem very likely; the West Indian planters and merchants very seldom traded to North America on their own account, and had no use for money in Boston or Philadelphia, however readily they might have grasped at money in London. The ship-owners in North America might empower their captains to draw on them for this purpose, but I cannot call to mind a single occasion when the permission was used.[3]

There was one more means of escape from the dilemma. If the owner was ready to have the proceeds of his outward cargo left behind for later shipment, or to let his captain take cash, light pay, sugar or anything else which would only half fill the vessel, then he could allow her to proceed on a salt voyage. Salt was to be had from three places in the Caribbean—Salt Tortuga and Bonaire off the Venezuela coast, and Turks Island between Hispaniola and the Bahamas. Salt Tortuga, which was already being frequented from Barbados in 1662,[4]

---

[1] J.D. to Lewis Galdy, 27 April 1717, Letter-Book of Jonathan Dickinson, p. 131, L.C.P.; to Joshua Crosby, 10 December 1717, *ibid*. The trouble seems to have been that light coins were officially valued higher in Jamaica than in Pennsylvania, so there was no inducement to export them.

[2] James Ball, Martinique, to Thomas Fayerweather, 12 June 1763, Thomas Fayerweather Commercial Papers, N.E.H. and G.S.

[3] Owners of the Schooner *Betsey* to John Hodges, September (?) 1761, Timothy Orne MSS., iv, 89, Essex Institute; Richard Derby to Captain Benjamin Bates, 28 June 1760, Derby Family MSS., vol. xxvii, *ibid*.

[4] Felix-Christian Spöri, in *Americanische Reiss-beschreibung nach den Caribes Inseln und Neu England* (Zürich, 1677), p. 66, says that after landing horses from Rhode

seems to have been the most popular, perhaps because it was uninhabited and there was nobody to be paid for the salt, though the vessels that went for it had to take with them special equipment, such as wheelbarrows, and additional hands at least from Barbados; at Turks Island and Bonaire one had to pay for the salt.[1] The salt ships sailed in convoy—on one occasion, as many as 35 of them[2]—from Barbados; this island was chosen, either because it was near the salt, or because, since it furnished hardly any molasses, the North Americans who frequented it were in danger of going home half full, or because, as the oldest colony, it was the most natural seat of the trade. It is not surprising that we hear most about salt voyages in the correspondence of Salem merchants, for Salem, as the seat of a fishing and fish-curing industry, needed salt. Messrs. Alexander Sandiford and Son, a merchant house of Barbados, said of the Salem traders, 'They generally send their vessels here twice a year, the first voyage they go home with salt, and the second they take home produce.'[3] But the salt voyages offered to everybody, not only to the Salem men, a convenient answer to the difficulties over the return cargo, and a skilful trader could combine a salt voyage with other schemes in order to use his vessel to the best advantage.

It would be unwise, however, to exaggerate the effect of these contrivances. Most North American captains knew that if they

---

Island at Barbados, 'darauf erklehrte sich unser Factoren, uns nach der insul Tortuga zuschicken, das Schiff daselbsten mit Saltz zuladen, und solches nach Neu-Engelland zuführen'. There were other islands called Tortuga, but none of them yielded salt.

[1] Timothy Orne and John Grafton to John Hodges, 3 January 1753, Timothy Orne MSS., ii, 77, Essex Institute; owners of the Schooner *Rebecca* to Captain Joseph Grafton, 17 February 1756, *ibid.*, iii, 15; in the Bancker Papers (N.Y.H.S.) there is the log book of the *King Solomon* which, in 1744, visited Salt Key (Turks Island) on her way home from Jamaica, picked up 1,000 bushels of salt at 7½d. per bushel in six days, and sailed home for New York. For cash (9d. per bushel) paid for salt from Bonaire, see the letter of G. Hopkins to Nicholas Brown and Co., 31 March 1765, papers of the Ship *Nancy*, Brown MSS., J.C.B.L.

[2] 'Here is 35 sail for tudu,' Joseph Grafton wrote to his owners from Barbados on 22 February 1759 (Timothy Orne MSS., x, 121, Essex Institute). It takes some guesswork to construe 'tudu' as Salt Tortuga, even in a letter from one of the habitually illiterate Salem captains; but the identification is pretty clear, for many people wrote 'Salt Tortuga' as 'Saltertudos' or even 'Salter Tudos'.

[3] A. Sandiford and Son to Pemberton and Edwards, 16 November 1773, Pemberton Papers, xxv, no. 139, H.S.P.

wished to sell, they must take what they could get in return. Sometimes they were at the mercy of planter-distillers who would give them rum when they wanted molasses,[1] at other times of sugar-drogers who took advantage of the competition for molasses to insist on selling so many casks of bad sugar with every boat-load.[2] Certainly, from the outcries in their letters home, one gets the impression that these captains—some of them simple souls, no doubt—were often the victims of circumstances or cunning, and glad to take home anything they could.

Sometimes their adversaries in these contests were planters, at other times merchants. The planters often held up the price of rum or molasses, relying on the keen competition of the buyers or on some special circumstance.[3] Whenever we read of the price 'breaking', we must understand by it some tacit or avowed collective bargain, bringing to an end a long deadlock between planters and buyers, and governing the first prices of the new season, perhaps all the prices of the year.[4] Less is said of concerted resistance by the buyers: the only definite plans for 'falling the price of molasses' were made at Surinam, where commercial conditions were rather peculiar;

[1] 'We are under a obbligation to sell for all sorts of produce for cannot altogether contract for molasses so that you'll have a considerable off a sortment tho' twill come dear to hand' (Gideon Manchester, Port Antonio, Jamaica, to Nicholas Brown and Co., papers of Brig *Sally*, 1764, Brown MSS., J.C.B.L.; see also the letter of Benjamin Wright, Savanna-la-Mar, Jamaica, to Rivera and Lopez, 29 February 1768, printed in *The Commerce of Rhode Island*, i, 225).

[2] Thomas Rogers, Cape Nicola Mole, St. Domingue, to C. and G. Champlin, 28 July 1771, printed *ibid.*, i, 375. On this occasion there were upwards of forty vessels waiting for molasses in the road at the Mole, so it was a sellers' market.

[3] They are often described as doing so in Antigua (Messrs. Birkett and Booth to John Reynell, 10 July 1751, 12 February and 14 June 1752, 3 March, 7 May and 27 October 1753, Coates-Reynell Papers, Boxes vi and vii, H.S.P.); sometimes also in Barbados (John Randall Phillips to Timothy Orne, 23 April 1767, Timothy Orne MSS., xii, 91, Essex Institute), in Jamaica (Benjamin Wright to Aaron Lopez and Co., 2 January 1768, printed in *The Commerce of Rhode Island*, i, 217; to Rivera and Lopez, 29 February 1768, *ibid.*, i, 225), and in Surinam (James Bowditch to Timothy Orne and Co., 5 November 1757 and 8 February 1758, Timothy Orne MSS., x, 82, 104, Essex Institute).

[4] It was still customary for the price of sugar to 'break' in this way (especially in war-time when the convoys came home) at London in the middle of the eighteenth century, but the phrase is not much used in the correspondence of the Pinneys at Bristol after 1783.

they will be discussed a little later, when the trade of that colony is examined.[1] But some tacit resistance there must have been very often, and the buyers had one strong card in their hand, for they usually provided the cask for molasses. The planters might refuse to sell at the price offered, but when their cisterns were full they would have no choice, and the buyers knew it.[2] This argument, however, did not apply to anything but molasses: the planters sold rum, sugar and everything else in cask of their own making.

The North American captain could not always lay his vessel alongside the planter's wharf; nor did the planter always choose to be responsible for delivering his produce at a port of common resort. At St. Lucia it seems to have been usual in 1774 to sell the outward cargo to the masters of sugar-drogers, or coasting vessels, who obliged themselves to pay in molasses at the current price in a few weeks' time.[3] Other captains, however, preferred to do their own sugar-droging. At Grenada, another new colony whose trade was still undeveloped, a Philadelphia captain found that 'molasses is not to be had without going to an outport' and that he could get no return cargo of any kind 'without taking a droger and going round the island where produce is in the greatest plenty, but they will not send it to market'. Finally he went off to Antigua in ballast, remarking, 'I could have got a load in this place provided I had inclined to have layd 3 or 4 months longer & run the risque of losing one half of it droging round the island, which I am determined not to do.'[4] In Surinam many of the northern captains lay in the river and sent agents, in punts or ships' boats with empty cask, up its branches to the plantations to buy molasses. Some of these agents were natives of the colony—we

[1] *V. infra*, pp. 113–17.

[2] John Hodges, Guadeloupe, to owners of Schooner *Betsey*, 13 January 1761, Timothy Orne MSS., xi, 98, Essex Institute; Silvanus Jencks, Paramaribo, to Nicholas Brown and Co., 14 January 1773, Brown MSS., J.C.B.L. For the buyer not to take the molasses when it was ready was, for this reason, an unpardonable offence (see the letter of A. P. Mendez, Savanna-la-Mar, to Aaron Lopez, 25 July 1768, printed in *The Commerce of Rhode Island*, i, 243).

[3] Daniel Bucklin, St. Lucia, to Nicholas Brown and Co., 20 March 1774, Brown MSS., J.C.B.L.

[4] John Harper to Thomas Clifford, 6, 10 and 21 March 1765, Clifford Correspondence, iv, 157, 159, 162, H.S.P.

hear of 'creoles' so employed.[1] More often the ship's crew were sent on these errands. The Browns of Providence were forever on the watch to see that they did their job properly. 'We have further to recommend', they wrote to Captain Whipple on 9 October 1764, 'that you in the strictest manner order your punt men to take no mel[s] but what is very good & for them to come emediatly of from the plantation after tasting the mel[s] if it should not be good & not to wait to be infegled & persuaded by the planters, further injoyn them to take none but good & if they do & that their private venters shall be fild out of the worst of it.' They repeated this threat the next year, and added that the puntmen should take a bottle of good molasses with them as a sample.[2] The purchase of molasses could be entrusted in this way to uneducated agents, for there were, to all intents and purposes, no recognized kinds or standards. That of sugar could not: we find another of the Browns' captains writing from Surinam: 'I can gitt sugar but as I am not able to goe myself to vew it I am afeard it will not answer so well as maloses.'[3]

The northern captains did not always deal directly with the planters like this. Even in Surinam we hear of them taking their 'turns' of molasses, presumably organized by a merchant or some other intermediary.[4] It must have been merchants, not planters, who threatened to land their molasses on St. Eustatius rather than sell it at the price current in the road.[5] The town agents of Barbados, who received (very often in payment of debts to themselves) the rum of numerous plantations, sometimes had so much control over the price of that article that it 'broke' according to the bargains they made. It was presumably to their interest to work it up as high as they could,

[1] I take it that 'I have got a creeall out with 12 hoxsats' means 'I have got a creole out with 12 hogsheads' in Thomas Morong's letter of 9 May 1753 to Timothy Orne and Co., Timothy Orne MSS, ii, 65, Essex Institute. There are other, and better spelt, references to this practice.

[2] Nicholas Brown and Co. to Abraham Whipple, 9 October 1764, papers of Brig *George*, 1764–5, Brown MSS., J.C.B.L.; to George Hopkins, 3 July 1765, papers of Ship *Nancy, ibid.*

[3] Esek Hopkins, Surinam, to Nicholas Brown and Co., 1 January 1767, papers of Sloop *Mary Ann, ibid.*

[4] These 'turns' could be bespoken beforehand (Nicholas Brown and Co. to Esek Hopkins, 25 and 28 October 1766, *ibid.*)

[5] George Dodge to Timothy Orne and Co., 7 August 1757, Timothy Orne MSS., x, 90, Essex Institute.

and they were sometimes accused of doing so. On one occasion, at least, they encountered a determined resistance among the buyers and had to ship rum to Philadelphia on their own account; their conduct was thought disloyal, since they were not only town agents but also factors, and in this capacity had vessels to dispatch with rum for their principals in North America.[1]

The merchants, however, did not always present themselves as the captains' antagonists in the market for produce. More often they would offer to help them to molasses, or even contract to deliver it. These undertakings were not always kept. It may be an accident, but most of the complaints of their infraction come from captains in the foreign colonies. Captain Israel Lovitt made an agreement with a merchant at Fort Royal, Martinique, in 1765 to load his vessel with molasses in thirty-six days: but four sail, or more, arrived shortly afterwards from North America, and began bidding so keenly for molasses that the price rose, and the merchant found it convenient to default on his promise; however, Captain Lovitt took him to law before the Governor, and made him fulfil it. In order to protect himself against such bad faith, at a time when all the northern captains were bidding against each other in order to get home with the first molasses of the new crop, Captain Cabot Gerrish made, the next year, the following agreement with one C. Savarry: 'I C. Savarry promish to deliver to Capt. Cabot Gerrish all the mollasses that is possible for me to get in the island of Martineco, and not to deliver any mollasses to any one else, untill the said Gerrish hath all he wants, and in case I should deliver direct or indirectly to any body else, any mollasses, I promish to pay to the said Gerrish one thousand livers p̄ tarse'—the molasses to be merchantable in quality and bought at the current price, and the tierces fair measure; in return for this, Savarry was to have five per cent of the value.[2]

---

[1] Thomas Gilbert, Barbados, to James Pemberton, 14 March 1772, Pemberton Papers, xxiii, 92, H.S.P.; John Hawkesworth to Pemberton and Edwards, 6 March 1774, *ibid.*, xxvi, 26; A. Sandiford and Son to the same, 2 May 1774, *ibid.*, xxvi, 65.

[2] Israel Lovitt to Jonathan Gardner and Co., 31 August, early October and 28 October 1765, Timothy Orne MSS., xii, 68, 70, Essex Institute; Cabot Gerrish to Orne and Cabot, 11 April 1766, *ibid.*, xii, 86, enclosing Savarry's agreement of 7 April, xii, 85.

From Surinam came the same complaints of bad faith. Perhaps the planters were not always to be blamed, for their creditors seized their molasses or dunned them into handing it over.[1] But the merchants, who were mostly creditors, should have had plenty of produce at command; indeed, they received their debts in it all over the West Indies. If they disappointed the northern captains, it was usually in order to get a better price. So, at least, the captains thought, and considered them as having no more principle or honour than highwaymen.[2]

Perhaps, at bottom, the captains had nobody but themselves to blame for this state of affairs. Certain seasonal fluctuations, no doubt, explain why it was really more difficult to get produce at some times than at others: at the fag-end of the year, before the new crop came in, there was very little of it at market and the price was high, so that some factors would rather wait for the new crop and, they hoped, for lower prices.[3] But the fundamental reason for high prices, even at crop-time, and the fundamental temptation to duplicity in the merchants was the intense competition of the buyers. The buyers themselves admitted it: they were always complaining that there were too many of them. Sometimes they put the blame on fishing vessels and privateers, who, having put in for molasses or rum as a mere incident in their voyages, were presumably too much in a hurry to stay and haggle in the approved professional manner.[4] More often, and more rightly, they blamed each other. 'There is severall here', wrote James Bowditch to his owners from Surinam, 'whose small purses will not admit of cheap melasses of which Jos. Wanton of Rhoad Island is one who has riseen the price of molasses from seven and a half to thirteen, the planters themselves say the price is too great and would willingly fix it at eight stivers.' Next spring he reported that 'the price of molasses is broke at eight & half stivers p̄

[1] James Bowditch, Surinam, to Timothy Orne and Co., 8 February 1758, Timothy Orne MSS., x, 104, Essex Institute.

[2] Esek Hopkins, Surinam, to Nicholas Brown and Co., 14 January, 9 and 22 March 1767, papers of Sloop *Mary Ann*, Brown MSS., J.C.B.L.

[3] Isaac Norris, for example, was always insisting on this (see, for example, his letter to Abel Bond, 5 December 1702, Letter-Books of Isaac Norris, ii, 4, H.S.P.).

[4] John Hodges, Guadeloupe, to owners of the Schooner *Betsey*, 12 March 1761 Timothy Orne MSS., xii, 22, Essex Institute.

gallon, thro' the falsity & inadvertency of Capt. Hoskins, who might have had the same at six & half stivers, which is fifteen hundred guilders damage to every man's voyage here, not excluding his own'.[1] At other times, the fault was not pusillanimity but impatience: it was in order to protect himself against the tricks of his rivals who were competing to be the first home with the produce of the first crop, that Captain Gerrish made the contract quoted above.[2] But most often nobody and nothing was at fault but the number of the competitors. Even four vessels were too many for the molasses procurable at one of the tiny outports of Guadeloupe, and forty for the fashionable commercial entrepot of Cape Nicola Mole.[3] They could not all be served: over and above the delays caused by the weather which interfered with the crop or the carting,[4] there were enormously long waits in harbour, 'worms eating the botom men the top'.[5] Probably these delays were worst at the small places: North Americans thought nothing of waiting as long as four or six months at Grenada, and it was reported in 1761 that there were so many New Englanders at Cayenne that some of them could not hope to get molasses in less than a year.[6] But even in the road of St. Eustatius, 1,500 hogsheads of molasses might be wanting, and that meant a long wait for somebody.[7]

[1] James Bowditch, Surinam, to Timothy Orne and Co., (?) 5 October 1757, 8 February 1758, Timothy Orne MSS., x, 90, 104, Essex Institute.

[2] *V. supra*, p. 108. Another instance of impatience to be gone, likewise at the beginning of the crop, is reported from Antigua in 1752 (Birkett and Booth to John Reynell, 3 March 1753, Coates-Reynell Papers, Box vii, H.S.P.).

[3] John Hodges, 'Baymelo', Guadeloupe, to owners of Schooner *Betsey*, 6 March 1760, Timothy Orne MSS., xii, 14, Essex Institute; Thomas Rogers, Cape Nicola Mole, to C. and G. Champlin, 28 July 1771, printed in *The Commerce of Rhode Island*, i, 375.

[4] Abraham Whipple, Surinam, to Nicholas Brown and Co., 6 July 1763, papers of Sloop *George*, 1763, Brown MSS., J.C.B.L.; P. Rolland, Cap François, to Aaron Lopez, 1 September 1773, Lopez MSS., iv, 18, Newport H.S.

[5] George Dodge, Fort Louis, Guadeloupe, to Timothy Orne and Co., 27 June 1759, Timothy Orne MSS., xi, 77, Essex Institute.

[6] John Harper, Grenada, to Thomas Clifford, 10 March 1765, Clifford Correspondence, iv, 159, H.S.P.; George Champlin, Surinam, to Messrs. Bowler and Champlin, 13 May 1761, Champlin Papers, Box 1732–1800, R.I.H.S.

[7] John Hodges, St. Eustatius, to owners of Schooner *Beaver*, 19 July 1758, Timothy Orne MSS., x, 96, Essex Institute.

II. TWO REPRESENTATIVE MARKET HISTORIES:
ANTIGUA AND SURINAM

Perhaps these generalities would be a little easier to comprehend if illustrated by the study of particular markets. Unhappily our information, though voluminous, is dispersed over nearly a dozen islands and more than a century. At two points, however, it concentrates itself enough to make some study of a particular market possible—at Antigua about 1747–66 and at the Dutch colony of Surinam 1760–70.

Antigua was an island of moderate, rather small plantations, producing very little besides sugar and rum; its chief port, St. Johns, was a political capital, and possessed a merchant class not comparable in wealth or activity with that of Kingston, Jamaica, of Bridgetown, Barbados, of St. Eustatius or Curaçao, but much more important than that of Nevis, Grenada or Montserrat. The pace of its commercial activity was probably quickened by its neighbourhood to one of these ports—St. Eustatius—and, indeed, being surrounded by islands of all nations, both its merchants and the transient captains who frequented it were conscious of the possibility of alternative markets. In nearly all these respects Surinam was quite different. It was a long way from the islands, and the strong currents on the coasts hindered its communication with the other Guiana colonies. There were merchants, but they by no means controlled all the trade of the colony, perhaps because it was so easy for the captains of transient vessels to send their ships' boats along the river to the planters' front doors. (If only it had been as safe to risk their boats on the surf of the lee shores, the captains could as well have shaken off their dependence on the merchants of Antigua.) It is probably no accident that more than half the extant letters from Antigua were written by resident factors, whereas at Surinam hardly a line comes from anybody but a transient captain.

The annexed table of prices at Antigua shows some interesting things. In the first place, all the prices before 1739 (and there are just enough of them to be significant) are remarkably lower than the later ones. This cannot be explained by the Molasses Act, which was not enforced and, if it had been enforced, might have turned the terms of trade between North America and the West Indies, but could not have raised the prices for both alike. It is more likely that the general rise in the price of sugar in England (which began in the War of Jenkins' Ear but continued until after 1763) dragged up that of sugar and rum in the islands and so enabled even their stationary populations to buy more North American produce and pay more for it. Nevertheless, if the terms of trade in the 1730's are compared with those of the later periods of peace (1749–55 and after 1763) it will be seen that the prices of northern produce in the island rose less, both absolutely and relatively, than those of rum and sugar. This, as I have said, cannot be due to the Molasses Act. It is more likely to be explained by the well-known fact that, for a time, production in North America increased faster than purchasing-power in the British West Indies; only later, and gradually, did the North Americans turn the terms of trade against the British sugar-planters by obtaining fresh markets for their produce and fresh sources of supply in the French islands.[1]

The effect of war on prices is fairly obvious. The prices of North American produce in the islands naturally had to be increased to cover the increased risk of capture. (It is noteworthy that the top price for flour occurred in 1741 when there was a large British fleet in the West Indies; but since most of that fleet was stationed at Jamaica, I doubt if it could have much effect on the price at Antigua.) What is not so obviously explained is the high price of sugar and rum, for these articles had to undergo the war risks after they left the islands, where the price ought to have been depressed. But the convoys to Europe (where the price was governed) were pretty safe; and the steady increase of consumption in Great Britain—indeed, in Europe—at this time probably gives the answer to this question.

It is harder to be sure about the effect of the weather. 1738, 1747, 1752, 1754, 1759 and 1765 were all years of bad crop at Antigua; that of 1753 was unusually good. It is probably not an accident that the price of sugar was usually pitched high in years of bad crop, for although (as I have said)

---

[1] *V. infra*, pp. 126–133, for the movements of prices in the North American ports.

the price of sugar in London depended on the production of the West Indies as a whole rather than that of any one island, yet the planters must naturally have been tempted to overrate their produce when their own crop fell short. The price of rum was not so evidently affected, though it, too, was generally high in a short crop. The effect of crops on the price of imported provisions is not clearly defined: if the weather which injured the sugar crop had at the same time injured the ground provisions on which the slaves relied, then the price of flour would go up; if it had not done so, then the planters, doleful about their balance-sheets and short of rum which they paid out as local currency, would buy no more flour than they could help. The price of lumber would be more directly affected. Short of a hurricane which would create a large demand for purposes of building, the consumption of lumber varied with the size of the crop to be put into cask; traces of this can be discerned in the table (for example, in the high price of staves in 1753, the low price in 1754, and the general tendency to fall every year about July or August, when the crop was finished).

The information about Surinam is not easy to compare with that about Antigua: it is almost all derived from the correspondence of Rhode Island or Salem captains, whereas the figures for Antigua come from that of Philadelphia merchants. New England's exports and imports in the West India trade were different from those of Philadelphia, and the only article in both lists is flour. (New England exported lumber, too, but there is very little information about the prices of lumber at Surinam in the prices current from which these figures are drawn.) Two of the exports given in the table, horses and candles, were valuable, and the principal import, molasses, was cheap and bulky—two to four pounds of flour would buy a gallon of molasses at Surinam, whereas it took ten to twenty pounds of flour to buy a gallon of rum at Antigua. No doubt this explains why the northern merchants could sometimes expect to buy two return cargoes with one outward cargo at Surinam, a thing which could never have happened at Antigua. The price of flour seems to have fluctuated a little more at Surinam than at Antigua, and the price of molasses at Surinam

ANTIGUA

		Flour, per cwt.	Mid. Bread, per cwt.	Staves, Red Oak, per th'sand	Staves, White Oak, per th'sand	Rum, per gallon	Sugar, per cwt.
1731	March	12–13s.	18s.	—	—	19–20d.	15–16s.
	April	12–13	18	—	—	18	—
	June	15	15–17	—	—	17½–18	19–20
	Sept.	12–14	15–17	—	—	—	20
1732	April	14–16	16–20	—	—	14–16	—
	Oct.	10	13	—	£14	18	15
1733	May	16	—	—	—	—	—
	Oct.	—	—	—	—	13½	—
1734	June	12–14	—	—	—	18	—
	July	12½	14	—	—	20	—
1738	Jan.	18	—	—	—	—	—
	March	18	—	—	—	—	—
(Bad crop)	April	12½	—	—	—	—	—
	May	15–16	—	—	—	—	—
1741	Aug.	35	40–45	—	—	—	—
	Sept.	28–30	35–40	—	—	—	—
1745	Nov.	—	—	—	—	30	—
1746	March	—	—	—	15–20	24	—
	Aug.	15–22	34	—	—	18	23
1747	May	18–22	35	—	—	30	35
	June	18–22	30	£6	15–16	36	35–7
(Bad crop)	July	18–22	35	—	14–16	39	35–6
	Aug.	15½–18	25–28	—	—	39	35
	Sept.	15½–20	—	10	20	36	35
	Oct.	18–24	30	12	23	36	30–35
1748	Jan.	24–28	28–35	—	—	—	—
1750	Sept.	20–24	28–30	—	—	34	30–34
1751	April	20–24	30	—	—	30	28–35
	May	18–24	28–31	—	9–12	30	28–35
	June	16½–20	28–31	—	9–10	30	34–35
	July	15–18	28–30	—	9–10	30	28–32
	Aug.	14–18	28–32	4	8½–10	30	27–28
(Hurricane)	Oct.	12½–20	—	4	9	30	32
	Dec.	12½–16	—	4½	8–9	36–39	—
1752	Jan.	12½–16	32–36	4½	9	38–40	30–35
	Feb.	12½–16	32–36	4–5	9	33–36	35

ANTIGUA

		Flour, per cwt.	Mid. Bread, per cwt.	Staves, Red Oak, per th'sand	Staves, White Oak, per th'sand	Rum per gallon	Sugar, per cwt.
	April	18–20	—	4–5	9	30	35
(Bad crop)	May	25	30–32	—	9½	30	40–43
	June	20–34	30–36	4–6	8–9½	36	42
	July	18–24	—	—	—	36	37–43
	Sept.	18–21	28–33	4–4½	8–9	—	—
	Oct.	18–23	28–32½	4–4½	8–9	37–38	40
	Nov.	18–23	30	3½–4	7½–9	39	—
	Dec.	17–22	28–32	4	8–9	42	—
1753	Jan.	14–18	28–30	4	7½–9	39	40
	Feb.	14–20	28	4½	10–12	—	—
	March	14–17	28–30	4½–5	10–12	39	—
	April	15–19	25–30	—	12	30–33	—
(Large, late crop)	May	13½–15	26	6	12½–14	24–27	—
	June	11–15	—	—	14	27	30–35
	Aug.	14–16½	—	4½–5	10–12	24	28–34
	Oct.	20	28	4	9	24–27	30–32
1754	Jan.	—	—	—	—	24	36–42
	March	—	—	—	—	28	40–45
	April	22	—	3½	8–10	33–36	40–45
(Bad crop)	May	18–22	—	—	—	30–36	40
	June	—	—	—	—	33	40–45
	Aug.	—	30	—	—	33	40
	Oct.	—	—	—	—	30	—
1755	Jan.	20–22	—	—	12	30	—
	April	17½	35	—	8	24	30
	Aug.	—	—	—	—	24	30
	Sept.	20	33	7–7½	9	23–24	30–33
	Nov.	30	36	—	—	—	—
1756	Jan.	26	—	—	10	24	—
	June	33	—	—	9	21–24	30–33
	Aug.	—	—	—	9	—	—
1757	Jan.	20–25	—	—	18–20	—	—
	Sept.	20	—	—	20	20	—
	Dec.	21–26	—	—	30	—	—
1758	Jan.	16	—	—	25	40	—
	April	22–26	—	—	25–28	—	—

ANTIGUA

		Flour per cwt.	Mid. Bread per cwt.	Staves, Red Oak, per th'sand	Staves, White Oak, per th'sand	Rum per gallon	Sugar per cwt.
	Sept.	20	—	—	—	—	—
1759	Feb.	20–26	—	—	—	40–42	—
(Bad crop)	March	20–26	—	—	25–28	40	40–45
1760	May	28–30	—	—	—	42	40
	July	35	—	—	—	48–51	40
	Aug.	21–25	—	—	—	48	40
1761	May	23–34	—	—	—	30	—
1764	Jan.	16	—	—	—	30	—
	June	14–16	—	—	—	24	30–35
1765	Jan.	18–26	—	5–6	12	28	22–34
	March	28–30	—	—	—	25	—
	April	20–30	—	—	15	24–25	30–35
(Late crop)	June	14–24	—	—	—	27–31	30–35
	July	—	—	—	—	28	30–35
	Aug.	20–24	—	—	10½	28	30–35
	Oct.	19–25	—	—	—	32	30–35
	Nov.	17–26	—	—	—	32	35–40
1766	Jan.	21–28	—	—	15–18	30	—
	March	20–27	—	—	12	24	36
	April	19–26	—	—	12–14	24	36
	May	17–25	—	—	9–12	23	30–36
	June	16½–24	—	—	9–12	22½–24	34–36
1767	Sept.	24–25	—	—	—	33	35–40

did so a little less than the price of rum at Antigua. The first of these two facts is perhaps to be explained by the consideration that Surinam was not surrounded, like Antigua, by alternative markets: perishable goods could not readily be exported or imported in order to keep the price steady. The comparative stability of the price of molasses may perhaps be accounted for by the fact that it was not exported to Europe, so its price did not depend on the expectations of a distant and sensitive market; also, perhaps, by the supposition that the planters did not care to haggle very hard about the price of an unregarded by-product. This, however, is not certain: the buyers frequently tried to lower the price by concerted action, and we cannot be sure that the sellers did not combine to keep it up.

Indeed, the chief interest of the Surinam correspondence is in the struggles between the captains, the planters and the merchants. Although, as I have said, the colony had not a large commercial class and the captains could deal direct with the planters, there were merchants who tried to thrust themselves between them as intermediaries. This was the point of the conflict of 1767, to which I have already referred: the merchants tried to discourage the captains from transacting business on their own account, by getting the Governor and Council to ordain that if they stayed behind after their vessels had sailed (which might be necessary for the recovery of debts or desirable because the same outward cargo would buy two successive return cargoes) they should pay the same taxes and do the same militia duty as resident merchants; and the planters retaliated by getting the Court of Police to order on the same day that the captains should sell horses direct to the planters without any intermediaries or put them up to auction.[1] But, though horses might be sold directly to the planters, I have the impression that flour and most other things were sold to the merchants. Captain Whipple of the *George*, in May 1763, sold his cargo to five different merchants, and expected them to load him in return.[2] On his next voyage his owners, who knew that three other vessels with similar cargoes were sailing from neighbouring ports for Surinam about the same time, advised him that if he arrived before them he should make a quick sale to the merchants, if after them, he should retail the cargo himself.[3] When the Rhode Island tobacco cartel was trying its hardest to keep up the price in Surinam, one of the Browns' captains wrote that he could have sold a few single hogsheads to the merchants at the cartel price, 'but if I sell to them single at 5 st. thay may keep me a longe time which may give them opertunity to suply a few of the plantations which wants most till thair comes in more and then it will fall.

[1] Notifications of 18 February 1767, with Esek Hopkins's note, Brown MSS., J.C.B.L.

[2] A. Whipple to N. Brown and Co., 24 May 1763, papers of Sloop *George*, 1763, *ibid.*

[3] N. Brown and Co. to A. Whipple, 16 September 1764, *ibid.*, 1764.

SURINAM

		Horses	Flour per cwt.	Spermaceti Candles per. lb.	Tobacco per lb.	Molasses per gallon
1734	June	60–120 guilders	2 stivers	6 stivers	—	3 stivers
1739	Sept.	40–60	1	—	—	5½–6
1752	Nov.	75	1	—	2 stivers	6½
	Dec.	—	—	—	—	6½
1754	June	70	1¾	—	2	10½–12½
	July	—	—	—	—	10½
1757	Oct.	—	5	20	—	—
	Nov.	—	—	—	3	11–12
1758	Feb.	—	5	—	4½	8½
	Dec.	140	2	25	6½	—
1760	July	—	—	—	—	8½
1761	May	—	—	—	—	10½–11
	July	—	—	—	—	8½
1763	April	150	3¾	25	2½	6½
	May	150	—	25	—	6½
	July	—	—	—	—	6½
1764	Nov.	145	—	26	5	6½
	Dec.	150	1½	26	5	6½
1765	Jan.	150	1½	26	5	—
1766	June	—	2–2¼	24–25	7¾	7
	Sept.	80	1½	24	3–4	7½
	Oct.	—	2¼	—	3½–4	—
1767	March	—	3½–5	—	—	6
	Aug.	—	—	—	—	8½
	Sept.	80–120	2½	22–24	3–3½	8½
1768	April	80	2½	—	2¼–2½	8½
	May	—	2–2½	26–28	—	8½
	Aug.	150	2–2½	23–26	2¼–2½	7½
1769	Jan.	—	2	—	3–3½	7–7½
	April	100	4	22	3	—
	May	—	—	—	—	7½
	June	—	2½	22	2¾–3¼	7½
1770	May	—	4	30	5	7½–8½
	Nov.	—	2	24–26	6–7	7
1771	Nov.	—	—	—	—	6
	Dec.	—	2¼–3	21–26	3–4	—
1772	July	—	4	—	—	7
1773	Jan.	—	4	30–36	2½–3	6
	March	—	—	—	—	7–7½
	April	—	—	—	—	10½
1774	Oct.	—	—	33–40	—	—

But thay have very little or none by them and I am in hops that in a few days the march[ts] must buy the whole if thay can't make me brack it.'[1]

This sounds as though the main tug-of-war, and most of the dealings, were between captain and merchant, not captain and planter. Likewise much of the molasses must have been procured through merchants. Whenever we read of 'turns' for molasses we may assume that merchants were concerned. Sometimes a captain would try to deal with the planters and find himself overborne by a merchant: in April 1769 Captain Simon Smith wrote to the Browns that he would have got all his molasses on board 'had it not bin for Mr Kenedy's ingageing to load the vessel menchend in my last, his intrust is so grate that he takes most all the molasses due to me from everybody'.[2] We have no means of knowing who were the captains' antagonists in their repeated (and mostly unsuccessful) attempts to 'fall the price of molasses' at Surinam by concerted action.[3] They may have been merchants or planters. It is certain that the trade cannot all have been in the hands of the merchants, though much of it was so. Direct relations between captains and planters were by no means unknown elsewhere— for instance, on the north side of Jamaica. But they seem to have been much commoner at Surinam than at Antigua.

III. THE DISPOSAL OF THE RETURN CARGOES

When a cargo of West India produce had been brought home to a North American port, it could be disposed of in more ways than one. An owner who also possessed a distillery or a sugar-refinery might transfer his goods straight from the one hand to the other. This only happened exceptionally: most often the return cargoes were destined to be sold on the market; but they

---

[1] Esek Hopkins to the tobacco cartel firms, 7 January 1767, papers of Sloop *Mary Ann, ibid.*

[2] Simon Smith to N. Brown and Co., 16 April 1769, papers of Brig *Sally, ibid.*

[3] This is most frequently mentioned in the Browns' correspondence: as they seem to have been the moving spirits in the tobacco cartel, it is not surprising that they were also keen on limiting buyers' competition at Surinam. See, for example, their instructions to Abraham Whipple, 9 October 1764, papers of Brig *George, ibid.*; his letters of 7 December 1764, 3 and 18 January 1765; Esek Hopkins to N. Brown and Co., 19 October 1766, *ibid.*

might be bartered or sold for cash or on credit, wholesale or retail.

The first step was to divide the cargo, where it did not all belong to the same person. Strictly speaking, this circumstance must have been almost universal, for the sailors of nearly every vessel had their own little 'privilege' cargoes, whether on their own or on somebody else's account. Little is known about the disposal of these private ventures; perhaps they were partly consumed in the seamen's own families. Freighters, if there were any, would presumably identify and claim their own goods. Most commonly, in the second half of the eighteenth century, the ship and cargo were owned by the same persons; but these might be partners, who would have to choose between dividing the goods to sell them separately and selling them in partnership to divide the proceeds. The latter course had the obvious advantage of avoiding competition between sellers.[1] It was usually taken—for example, by the Browns of Providence, who made up their partnership accounts for all completed voyages on the first day of January each year.[2] Other partners, however, preferred to divide before selling: for instance, Joshua Hempstead of New London, who held a share in a number of small vessels in the West India trade, usually spent a day, after their return, in dividing the cargoes; his part he peddled in the neighbouring towns, especially on Long Island.[3]

[1] This is illustrated by a letter from Isaac Norris to Richard Hill, 8 September 1705, apparently referring to transactions in rum: 'Yesterday they ask't me 2/8 wch I refus'd and now I can hear of none under 2/10 ready money, the Comp^a have agreed to buy out one anoth^r so that they have drawn into few hands & combin'd as to price. I could not find any buy^r in way but Tho. Grayham & to prevent his injuring my buying sold him 200 gall^o at 2/8 and am catcht in it unless more come in or these abate' (Isaac Norris Letter-Book, iii, 94, H.S.P.). It is interesting to notice that Norris immediately responded to a restriction of sellers' competition by restricting that of the buyers. In general, restriction of competition among buyers or sellers of West India produce must have been very unusual. There were too many sellers and the markets were too near each other. 'I think', wrote Benjamin Mason of Newport on 1 May 1773, 'a combination about keeping up the price of moll^s can never stand, without they will keep a general stock & lend each other money as they may want' (Brown MSS., J.C.B.L.). The distillers or refiners may have combined, but could not, even so, control a market where the industrial uses for raw sugar and molasses were supplemented by a great demand for private consumption.

[2] Journals of Obadiah Brown, R.I.H.S.　　　　[3] See his *Diary*, *passim*.

The sale of West India produce very often took the form of barter. Indeed, in the earliest days, sugar and tobacco from the West Indies may almost be said to have served as currency in New England; but never quite so much as in the islands themselves, at any rate for large transactions, for, although some contracts stipulated for payment in sugar or tobacco without qualification, many more fixed a money valuation for the sugar or tobacco itself, or provided that it should be delivered at the current price in money or as for bills of exchange, thus showing that the produce was not truly currency though it was a means of payment.[1]

For many years—indeed, down to the age of the American Revolution—rum and molasses figured in every kind of barter transaction. Among the articles for which they were exchanged, in whole or part payment, were bread, tobacco, spermaceti candles, head-matter (the raw material of candles), hats, land, ships, and dwelling houses. For any constructional work which required the employment of much labour, rum and molasses necessarily formed part of the payment because the contractor had to dispense these articles constantly to the workmen. For instance, in 1749, Andrew Webster, of New Hampshire, husbandman, contracted to build a schooner for Timothy Orne and his partners, the price to be paid half in cash, half in West India goods. For building a house on Orne's farm, three years later, Benjamin Deland of Danvers received rather more than two-thirds of his payment in West India goods, besides 10 gallons of rum and 10 lb. of sugar which Orne was to pay, doubtless as a *pourboire* for the workmen.[2] For the same reason the account of Matthew Manchester with the Governor and Company of a furnace in which the Browns were interested consists in part of innumerable disbursements of rum, presumably to the workmen.[3] In 1737 a merchant of Louisbourg refused to sell a vessel for 60 hogsheads of rum and 60 of molasses but would have taken indigo, another West India staple.[4] The Browns of Providence paid for a sloop in 1764 in

[1] *Aspinwall Notarial Records*, pp. 20, 282; *Suffolk Deeds*, i, 122; iii, 324.
[2] Timothy Orne MSS., vols. i and ii, Essex Institute.
[3] Brown MSS., J.C.B.L.
[4] Peter Faneuil to Thomas Kilby, 12 August 1737, Letter-Book of Peter Faneuil, N.E.H. and G.S.

merchantable molasses at 1s. 8½d. lawful money per gallon, 300 gallons on demand, 900 gallons on laying her deck, and the rest when she was finished.[1]

Nothing was too large to be paid for in rum and molasses—or too small. Obadiah Brown once paid an insurance premium in molasses, and there exists among the Brown manuscripts the account-book of an apothecary who took West India goods, as well as pepper, iron, hay and tobacco, in payment for his drugs and prescriptions; some of the West India goods he retailed in smaller quantities.[2] One of the Browns tipped people in molasses for minor services.[3]

Besides these transactions, there were others in which distillers exchanged rum for its raw material, molasses, and refiners exchanged loaf sugar for raw. These will be examined later.

The general shortage of cash was the chief reason for all this. Far more people on the continent of North America had rum and molasses to disburse than large sums of cash. Conversely, industrialists like the Browns would try to buy West India produce with their own manufactures rather than pay cash for it, even if this meant paying a higher notional price: thus, in October 1763 when they wanted 20 hogsheads of molasses, they would rather buy it at 38s. per gallon for payment in spermaceti candles (valued at 56s. per lb.) than get it at 35s. for cash payment in three months.[4] Such barter was often competitive: when Benjamin Mason, on behalf of the Browns, tried to exchange candles at 56s. for molasses at 38s., he found him-

---

[1] Papers of Sloop *Flying Fish*, 1764, Brown MSS., J.C.B.L.

[2] 'Mary Vanderlight's book', *ibid*. This was almost certainly kept by Nathaniel Sweeting.

[3] 'Blotter no. 3', *ibid*.

[4] Nicholas Brown and Co. to Benjamin Mason, 31 October 1763, *ibid*. The difference between cash and barter prices was often much greater than this: Jonathan Dickinson of Philadelphia explained to his West Indian brother-in-law that 'We barter goods for staves and hoops but we cannot sell for money unless we would dispose of our goods at the rates of others, not ⅓ so good' (J.D. to Isaac Gale, 10 May 1721, Letter-Book of Jonathan Dickinson, p. 379, L.C.P.). The explanation was one which a West Indian would readily understand, for the difference between cash prices and sugar prices was much greater in the islands: in February 1720 at St. Kitts bohea tea was sold at 21/- per lb. in cash or 56/- per lb. in sugar. (Account-book of (?) Alexander Wooddrop, Library of Congress, Ac. 741.)

self outbidden by another dealer who offered candles at 55s. for
molasses at 40s.[1] These bargains were complicated and sometimes highly speculative: for instance, Moses Brown advised his
brothers to accept an offer of rum for candles, because he
believed that rum would not fall and candles would; presumably the other party to the bargain thought otherwise.[2]
The complication is increased, for the historian at least, by the
fact that the same persons were by no means on the same side
of every bargain: thus the Brown brothers, whom the transactions just described reveal as trying to buy molasses and rum
with candles, often bought head-matter or tobacco with
molasses and rum, and again, at other times, managed to sell
molasses and rum for cash which they paid to the tobacco-
growers. Their father James Browne behaved in just the same
way: sometimes he had exchanged country produce for West
India goods, at other times *vice versa*.[3] He may have had a
reason for this, besides the general shortage of cash: he was a
small, up-country trader, on the very edge of the main commercial current (for Providence was then little more than a
village) and he had little capital or knowledge of market conditions; small wonder, then, that he preferred a barter bargain
at stated prices[4] to standing the hazard of the Newport or
Boston market as buyer or seller.

The scarcity of hard cash, which made so many barter
transactions necessary, also made sales on credit common—but
perhaps in slightly different circumstances. It is probably no
accident that most of the former come from places like Providence, New London, or the early Philadelphia, in close touch
with the hinterland, while most of the latter come from places
like Newport or New York, where money was concentrated and
long-distance trade brisk.

There seems to have been no standard length of credit for
sales of West India produce. John van Cortlandt, the New

[1] Benjamin Mason to Nicholas Brown and Co., 17 February 1764, Brown MSS.,
J.C.B.L.
[2] Moses Brown to Nicholas Brown and Co., 14 September 1769, *ibid.*
[3] See the *Letter Book of James Browne, passim*, especially pp. 23, 39, 45.
[4] In fact the prices were not always stated; but I have the impression that when
he left it to the recipient to fix the price (e.g. in his letter to Mr. Gibbs of Newport,
4 March 1735/6, *ibid.*, p. 21), he was usually addressing a creditor.

York sugar-refiner, sometimes sold his loaf sugar at six months'
credit, but at other times refused to give more than three, on
the ground that he had to buy his raw sugars for cash; but this
argument was not quite true for, at least once, he bought a
large parcel for payment in four months.[1] The different goods
in the trade varied in their power to command cash: West
India produce in general would sell for cash more easily than
flour, but molasses, which was described as a 'constant spend-
money', would command cash in New York or Boston even
better than rum;[2] in a minor centre like Baltimore, a merchant
would not undertake to sell a cargo even of molasses for cash,
though he could 'make it turn round well enough'.[3] Credit
prices differed from cash prices much less than barter prices:
John van Cortlandt sold his loaf sugar for 13½d. per lb. cash,
14d. per lb. credit, and the New York distillers, about the same
time, sold rum at 2s. 1d. per gallon for cash and at 2s. 2d. for
two months' credit.[4]

Even the records of a cash transaction may be misleading
unless we have full information about the quality of the goods.
One might suppose that so humble an article as molasses would
be the same the whole world over, unless it was out of condition; but this was not so. The distillers liked it substantial,
but were indifferent to the appearance, while the retailers
would give an extra penny or two for a good colour.[5] (Exactly
the same difference prevailed in the sugar trade: the grocers

[1] John van Cortlandt to I. Younghusband, 15 December 1763; to Messrs.
Duncan and Pugh, 17 March 1766; to Captain Leycraft, 25 July 1766, John van
Cortlandt Letter-Book, N.Y.P.L.

[2] G. G. Beekman to Committee of War, Rhode Island, 20 May 1755, Beekman
Letter-Book, N.Y.H.S.; Henry Lloyd, Boston, to Aaron Lopez, 24 December
1755, Letters of Boston Merchants, 1732–66, MS. I, 1,1,1, p. 24, Boston Public
Library.

[3] William Lux to Darby Lux, 11 April 1765, Letter-Book of William Lux,
N.Y.H.S.

[4] G. G. Beekman to J. and W. Russel, 29 April 1765, Beekman Letter-Book,
ibid. There was, of course, an even greater difference between wholesale and
retail prices. In the day-books of Witter and Styles (*ibid.*), which disclose numerous
transactions between 1753 and 1761, the retail selling price of rum seems to have
been normally 20 to 40 per cent above the wholesale price.

[5] John Watts, New York, to Nicholas Brown and Co., 3 and 17 July 1769,
Brown MSS., J.C.B.L.; G. G. Beekman to Thomas Freebody, 25 January
1758, Beekman Letter-Book, N.Y.H.S.; to Solomon Fowler, 5 December 1763,
ibid.

went for colour, the refiners for strength.[1]) Moreover the distillers distinguished between the molasses of the different sugar colonies, and tried to mingle them in the right proportions: thus Thomas Cranston of Newport wrote to the Browns, 'I now stand in need of four hhds of Surranam mollasses, I have worked French so long that three or four fatts calls loud for some of that sort.'[2] It is clear, then, that 'a gallon of molasses' was not always the same thing, and all kinds did not command the same price.

The rum of the different islands varied in character much more distinctly than their molasses—to say nothing of the rum distilled in North America, which was really a different article whose competition must be treated separately.[3] Certain rums had a special local popularity—for example, Antigua rum in New York.[4] In Philadelphia, Barbados rum was originally preferred to that of Jamaica for its cheapness, but in time Jamaica rum came to be the chief drink in the public houses of the town.[5] French rum, which began to enter the New York market about 1750, was scarcely better esteemed there than that of New England.[6] Besides the various rums, Jamaica and Barbados produced 'spirit', distilled straight from the cane juice instead of molasses and skimmings. This was a superior article, used in punch, and much costlier than common rum.[7] So a transaction in rum is by no means self-explanatory, unless we know what kind of rum it was.

[1] See my book, *A West India Fortune*, p. 190.

[2] Thomas Cranston, Newport, to Nicholas Brown and Co., 28 November 1770, Brown MSS., J.C.B.L.

[3] *V. infra*, pp. 133-4.

[4] W. and S. Franklin, New York, to Thomas Clifford, 14 and 30 July 1766, Clifford Correspondence, iv, 242, 253, H.S.P.; Thomas Clifford to Samuel Smith, 6 August 1766, *ibid.*, xxvii, 456.

[5] Isaac Norris to Jonathan Dickinson, January–February 1699/1700, 30 May 1707, Isaac Norris Letter-Books, i, 135; iv, 73–4, H.S.P.; Jonathan Dickinson to Isaac Gale, 2 May 1715, Letter-Book of Jonathan Dickinson, pp. 17–18, L.C.P.

[6] G. G. Beekman to Southwick and Clark, 3 August 1762, Beekman Letter-Book, N.Y.H.S.

[7] G. G. Beekman to Thomas Clifford, 7 August 1766, Clifford Correspondence, iv, 254, H.S.P. According to Beekman, the Barbados spirit was esteemed above that of Jamaica, though not so strong. In May and December 1773 the Pembertons bought Jamaica spirit at 4/4 and 3/11 per gallon respectively, West India rum at 3/4 and 3/2 respectively, North American rum at 2/3 and 2/5 respectively (Pemberton Papers, xxv, nos. 9, 156, H.S.P.).

Less is heard of the varieties of sugar, probably because few
residents in North America could afford to be particular about
the quality of their sugar; many of them used very little of it at
all, being content to sweeten their food more cheaply with
molasses, or at best with the coarsest sugars. Good muscovado,
as Jonathan Dickinson wrote in 1717, 'will not yeild a propor-
tionate advance with corser sugars of which sort from Barbados
& the Carribbee Isles here comes a full supply'.[1] The great
wars of the next generation, however, familiarized the North
Americans with the superior French sugars, brought in by the
illicit traders or as prizes by the privateers, and the growth of
sugar-refining on the continent must have brought loaf sugar
into more frequent use; so it is not surprising to find G. G.
Beekman of New York telling a correspondent in 1765 that
none but the best sugar would sell in the New York market, the
inferior sorts could only be disposed of to the refiners.[2]

IV. PRICES

The many varieties of sugar and rum, with their corresponding differences of price, make the study of prices from the
records of transactions an almost impossible task: only for
molasses could it be attempted, even if the evidence existed at
all. Fortunately the newspaper prices current seem to be, on
the whole, a reliable guide: although there are cases which look
as though the quotations had been negligently repeated from
one number to the next for some weeks and then suddenly
brought up to date with a jerk,[3] there are many more in which
they appear to have been correct, when compared with the
prices current which merchants gave each other in their private
letters (though, of course, there is no means of knowing that the
merchants did not copy these prices from the newspapers themselves). Unfortunately, few of the newspapers came into being

---

[1] J.D. to Isaac Gale, 7 September 1717, Letter-Book of Jonathan Dickinson,
p. 142, L.C.P.

[2] G. G. Beekman to S. Townshend, 4 April 1765, Beekman Letter-Book,
N.Y.H.S.

[3] As, for example, when the *American Weekly Mercury*, having quoted muscovado
sugar at 30 to 45/- ever since 26 January 1720, suddenly altered it on 18 August
1720 to 29–35/- at which price it remained until 13 December.

before 1720, nor did they all regularly publish such quotations. There is the further difficulty of dealing with prices in a currency whose value changed fast or far. But if we take a reliable paper like the *American Weekly Mercury*, quoting in a relatively stable currency like that of Pennsylvania, we can learn something of the secular movements and the seasonal fluctuations.[1]

The impression made by the secular movements is very much what might be expected, for these movements were, on the whole, parallel with those of the London sugar markets. There was a rapid descent from high prices before and, still more, after the Peace of Utrecht into the slump of the 1720's and the early 1730's. West India rum, which touched 4s. the gallon in March 1720, December 1722, and from November 1726 to January 1727, only reached 3s. on three occasions in the next twelve years (in October 1729, August-October 1731, and September-October 1734). A slow rise began in 1734. In 1739, when the War of Jenkins' Ear broke out, the price had been at 2s. 1d. or 2s. 2d. for more than a year. Molasses, on the other hand, had risen rather more; 1s. 6d. per gallon had been a middling good price in the 1720's, but from July 1734 to the outbreak of the war a lower price was only quoted twice. It is less easy to make sense of the prices of sugar, for very wide margins are quoted, and the quotations remain stereotyped for so long that their truth is questionable. But here, as in rum, there seems to have been a fall about 1720, and very low prices were usual in the early 1730's—the lowest of all, at the end of 1733, can probably be attributed to forestalling imports of French sugars by merchants who believed that the Molasses Act would interrupt the trade with the foreign sugar colonies.

The effect of war stands out very clearly. The prices of all West India goods rose for a few months after the outbreak in 1739, but the great increase took place in the latter part of 1741. West India rum was never below 2s. 9d. for the next five years, and if molasses flagged a little in 1743 and early 1744, it soared above 2s. when the French came into the war,

---

[1] The history of these prices can be followed in Arthur H. Cole, *Wholesale Commodity Prices in the United States, 1700–1861* (Cambridge, Mass., 1938) and in Anne Bezanson, Robert D. Gray and Miriam Hussey, *Prices in Colonial Pennsylvania* (Philadelphia, 1935).

and stayed there for years. This was not because the trade with
the French sugar colonies was interrupted: on the contrary, the
North Americans frequented them in war-time as never before.[1]
It was the high war risks and costs, the heavy demand of men-
of-war and privateers for rum, and the widespread, if rather
oddly distributed increase of purchasing power derived from
war-time prosperity, that made this difference. The price of
sugar rose too, but did not benefit so clearly from the war:
though there were some periods, such as the first part of 1744,
when it was very high indeed, at others (for example, for most
of 1743) it was not as high as it had often been in peace-time.
The reason for this is not very clear. War risks had a slightly
depressing influence on the price of sugar in the islands, where
the heavier freights and insurance premiums had to be deducted
from the probable European market price. This affected the
French sugar colonies much more than the British, whose trade
was better protected,[2] and perhaps explains, in part, why it
was worth the Americans' while to buy so much of it in war-
time; but it affected the British colonies too. The price of sugar
in North America would be kept down, not only by these
increased imports of French sugar but also by the sale of prize
goods,[3] which the northern colony privateers generally brought
into their home ports. This would affect sugar more than rum,
for French and Spanish ships carried little rum home to
Europe: as John Waddell wrote from New York in 1756, 'I am
inform'd that some vessells that are expected here will bring
less sugars and more rum by reason of so many sugar prizes
lately brought to this port.'[4] Even though normal imports from
the British colonies might be thus discouraged, the net increase
in the quantity of raw sugar at the North American markets
must have been great. This would keep the price down, and

[1] See my book, *War and Trade in the West Indies*, chapter ix.

[2] *Ibid.*, pp. 328–30.

[3] The importers of prize goods could not well avoid paying the duties imposed
by the Molasses Act, which hardly any other importers ever paid. (The table given
on p. 275 of F. W. Pitman, *The Development of the British West Indies* shows that considerable sums were paid on prize sugars during the War of the Austrian Suc-
cession.) But even with this disadvantage prize sugars undersold the normal
imports.

[4] John Waddell to Thomas Wharton, 6 December 1756, Wharton Papers,
Box i, H.S.P.

incidentally encourage the refining industry.[1] The only thing to counteract this effect on prices was the speculative re-export of sugars to Europe, which was particularly brisk, especially at New York, in the later years of the Seven Years War.

The decade 1730-40 was a turning point in the history of European sugar prices: they never returned to the low levels of 1730 until after the battle of Waterloo. The impulse given to the prices of West India produce in North America was less permanent. In Philadelphia the rise of sugar prices roughly kept pace with that of flour prices until 1763, when the ratio began to fall a little. The same thing is true of molasses and rum, but the fall after 1763 was greater. In New York from 1749 to 1775, imports, of which the most important were sugar, rum, and molasses, depreciated slightly in terms of native products. In Boston the movement was most pronounced. From 1720 to 1735 a bushel of wheat exchanged for three and a half to four gallons of molasses; by 1748 it fetched only two gallons. From that point molasses began to fall in terms of wheat, slowly until 1763, much faster from that year until 1775, when a bushel of wheat would bring five gallons of molasses or even more.[2] Probably the earlier appreciation of West India produce was caused not so much by the war as by the discrepancy between the rate at which production expanded on the continent and in the British sugar colonies; the balance was righted after 1748 by the ever-increasing intercourse between British North America and the French sugar colonies, which provided new markets for northern produce and new supplies of sugar and molasses.

When we study the lesser fluctuations of prices it is necessary to remember how small and poor most of the markets were, especially in the first century of colonization. They were very easily glutted with the minor products—Cadwallader Colden reported to a friend in 1714 that there was enough limejuice in Philadelphia to serve the place two years.[3] Perhaps this is one

[1] 'All the sugar houses supplys themselves from the prizes, tho' they have such choice of other sugars' (Waddell Cunningham to Leggs, Hyde and Co., 31 December 1757, Letter-Book of Greg and Cunningham, N.Y.H.S.).

[2] Cole, *op. cit.*, pp. 14-16, Appendix A, pp. 118-19; Bezanson, *op. cit.*, pp. 180-1, 188-91, 212-14.

[3] C.C. to Jacob Valverde, 23 June 1714, *Colden Papers*, i, 15.

K

reason why we read so little about these minor products in the merchants' correspondence: they did not find it worth while to deal in them. A little sugar, too, was enough for early Newport or Philadelphia.[1] Even of rum and molasses a few sloop-loads coming in together were enough to 'pall' the Philadelphia market. As late as 1766 the resident merchants of that town were not above complaining of the transient captains for spoiling the market in rum, as if the place had been the capital of a paltry island.[2]

The smallness of the particular markets would not matter so much if the coastwise trade was so well developed that the whole coastline could be considered as a single market. It will be evident, from details to be given later, that considerable quantities of West India goods were carried up and down the coast in all directions, and that this sometimes affected the prices.[3] The markets in Maryland were long ruled by those of Philadelphia, those of Long Island were subject to influence from Newport and New York. Even between the main centres themselves, the merchants were constantly comparing prices current, and from time to time speculative consignments made a real difference to the markets. Yet this difference was seldom stated in so many words.

The prices in Europe must have had some indirect effect in North America, for it was, in all probability, the general and permanent improvement in the prices of West India produce in Europe that raised the North American prices likewise. But we seldom hear of the European prices as affecting the markets at a particular conjuncture, and then only in special circumstances, as in the speculative boom in the re-export of prize sugars at the height of the Seven Years War.[4] On the other hand the actual or expected prices of produce in the islands were quite often mentioned as determining the prices to the northward;

[1] Isaac Norris to Jonathan Dickinson and John Askew, 24 August 1699, Isaac Norris Letter-Book, i, 51, H.S.P.; Peleg Sanford to John King, n.d. (1666–7), *Letter-Book of Peleg Sanford*, p. 22.

[2] S. and J. Smith to Thomas Avery, 24 February, 25 April 1766, Letter-Book of S. and J. Smith, Library of Congress.

[3] *V. infra.*, pp. 157–61.

[4] Thomas Clifford to Isaac Cox, 26 July 1760, Clifford Correspondence, xxvii, 99, H.S.P.

but the influence of the markets at the source of supply is not the same thing as that of competing centres of distribution.[1]

The influence of the seasons upon the markets for West India goods was notable in two respects. The haymaking and the harvest increased and mobilized human thirst, and so created a demand not only for rum but also for molasses which could be turned into rum or brewed into various sorts of beer. 'My demand with my country customers', wrote a Boston distiller, 'is so large now in hay time that I cannot distill fast enough for them, & I have tryed to borrow a hogshead in Boston but it is so quick for ready cash that I have not been able.'[2] But the great influence was that of the Philadelphia harvest: Philadelphia was the gateway to the largest and richest corn-growing country in North America, whose thirst made itself felt as far north as Newport, Rhode Island.[3] Its effect upon the markets nearer home was for long a matter of common knowledge. I have not discovered in the merchants' correspondence an earlier reference to it than 1699,[4] but after that they are common. John Reynell, for example, reminds one of his captains in 1755, 'that unless thou art here before harvest it will be a considerable disadvantage in the sale of the rum.'[5] Ten years or so later, Messrs. S. and J. Smith explained why the distillers bought so little molasses at the beginning of June: the 'harvest run' would be over by the 20th of the month, and the distillers would only buy as much as they could turn into rum before that date, after which the price would drop.[6]

The price statistics, such as we have them, do not altogether confirm these beliefs: though there were years, such as 1741

[1] Isaac Norris to Jonathan Dickinson, 12 April 1703, Isaac Norris Letter-Book, ii, 44, H.S.P.; John Reynell to David Fogo, 7 August 1755, Reynell Letter-Book, i, 46, *ibid*.

[2] John Hunt, Boston, to Timothy Orne, 23 July 1752, Timothy Orne MSS., x, 37, Essex Institute.

[3] Benjamin Mason of Newport, explaining on 7 June 1773, to the Browns of Providence that there was no demand for rum, said 'the Phila vessels are gone for the harvest tripp' (Brown MSS., J.C.B.L.).

[4] Isaac Norris to Richard Poor, 1 June 1699, Isaac Norris Letter-Book, i, 1, H.S.P.

[5] J.R. to Captain Nathaniel Donnell, 5 April 1755, Reynell Letter-Book, iii, 31, H.S.P.

[6] S. and J. Smith to N. Holmes, 7 and 13 June 1766, Letter-Book of S. and J. Smith, Library of Congress.

and 1744, when the prices rose in the early summer, there were others, such as 1720 and 1721, when they fell, and many more in which nothing in particular happened. These figures reveal much more clearly a quite different movement—the rise in the autumn and early winter. There were probably several reasons for this rise, but it was due above all to the expectation that winter would interrupt communications: the rivers would probably freeze in the new year, so that further supplies were not likely to reach the ports for some time, and the up-country customers bought largely in order to stock their cellars before the roads became too bad.[1] This seasonal movement, like the other, is heard of as early as 1699.[2]

The markets in North America were not only very small at first, but also very poor. The tobacco and rice planters of the south, among whom money or at least London credit abounded, might perhaps buy without looking too closely at the price, but the people of the northern and middle colonies had to count every penny, and bought when goods were cheap. 'I have always observed', Isaac Norris wrote, 'that when rum is dear we do not sell $\frac{1}{4}$ of that quantity as at other times . . . for our people are not Virginians to have it cost w^t it will.'[3] 'It's poor mean stinke but's spirit', wrote Jonathan Dickinson about some Barbados rum, '& our country people are for that that is cheapest', and again, 'as all men retract their liveing most people here are for the lowest prices except some few that know that good molasses will with lesser quantity make better drink'.[4]

This parsimony had several obvious results. Alternative products, such as sugar and molasses, or rum and cider, competed keenly with each other. Undoubtedly the chief thing that limited the consumption of sugar was the cheapness of molasses. Not only rum but also molasses was lessened in value at Phila-

---

[1] James Bickham, Lancaster, to Thomas Wharton, 28 October, 18 and 25 November 1754, Wharton Papers, Box i, H.S.P.

[2] Isaac Norris to James Mills, 9 October 1699, Isaac Norris Letter-Book, i, 90, H.S.P. (Arthur H. Cole, *op. cit.*, pp. 90–1, suggests that after the mid-century the seasonal variations in the prices of molasses and rum at Philadelphia and Boston became harder to perceive.)

[3] Letter quoted in preceding footnote.

[4] J.D. to E. Gomersall, 10 May 1721; to Isaac Gale, 10 May 1721; Jonathan Dickinson Letter-Book, pp. 377, 380, L.C.P.

delphia by a good apple crop, for the cider was commonly distilled into spirits.[1] An occasional importation of spirits from England had the same effect: the drink might not be good, but it was cheap, and therefore interfered with the price of rum.[2] But the best example is the competition of New England and West India rum—later, of Philadelphia, New York, Charleston and Baltimore rum with both of them.

V. THE PROCESSING INDUSTRIES

When 'rum' is mentioned in the correspondence of North Americans before 1700, it is almost always West India rum that is meant. The northern distilleries did not begin to compete seriously before 1713,[3] and even then vast quantities of rum were still imported from the islands. As it was a better article, it commanded a better price, but, as Thomas Clifford pointed out, 'when there is so much difference in the price [as between 3/9½ and 2/6] the country buys the cheapest sort and makes a little West India serve'.[4] Thus the normal competition which the distilleries on the mainland afforded by their very existence, tended to encourage the shipment of molasses rather than rum from the islands: for example, William Lux of Baltimore, finding that 'people seem to be more inclin'd to encourage the country rum as it is so much cheaper', decided to reorganize his system of West India trade and bring home molasses.[5]

This led, as one might expect, to a marked change in the relation between the price of West India rum and that of molasses: the latter, being in greater demand, rose in price relatively to the former. Many of the early quotations (for example, in Isaac Norris's letter-books about 1700) show rum at 170 to 220 per cent of the price of molasses; the ratio in the winter and spring of 1719–20 was never (according to the *American Weekly Mercury*) less than two to one, and on occasion,

---

[1] Jonathan Dickinson to John Lewis, 7 November 1715; to Jonathan Gale, 7 June 1718, *ibid.*, pp. 55, 198.

[2] John Watts to Francis Clarke, 2 January 1762, *Letter Book of John Watts* (N.Y.H.S.), p. 6; Richard Smith, Philadelphia, to Richard Derby, 20 April 1762, Derby Family MSS., vol. xii, Essex Institute.   [3] *V. supra*, p. 51.

[4] Thomas Clifford to Jonas Maynard, 17 March 1762, Clifford Correspondence, xxvii, 200, H.S.P.

[5] W.L. to William Sanders, 22 July 1764, Letter-Book of William Lux, N.Y.H.S.

three to one. That, admittedly, was unusual in the 1720's, but 180 per cent was not. In the middle and late 'thirties 140 per cent was about the average, though it rose somewhat in the War of Jenkins' Ear, when the demand for ready rum must have been brisk. The figures, certainly, are full of eccentricities—the gap widened and narrowed, for example it fell from 1s. 6d. in October 1734 to 4d. in May 1735, from 1s. 6d. in January 1745 to 8d. in June; on the whole, molasses, the raw material, neither rose so fast as rum in the harvest and early winter, nor fell so fast in the slack season. Most of these fluctuations doubtless arose from chance variations of supply; a few, perhaps, from concerted attempts of the distillers to keep off the market for molasses, which would lower its price without affecting that of rum.

Throughout the fluctuations, however, there was a general tendency to narrow the gap between the prices of molasses and rum; and this must, no doubt, be attributed to the rise of the distilleries on the mainland which not only kept up the price of molasses by maintaining the demand, but also kept down the price of West India rum by furnishing a cheap and nasty substitute. Of the cheapness there can be no doubt. Unlike West India rum, which was not usually, except at seasons of slump, less than 50 per cent above the price of molasses, New England rum was usually only 2d. to 6d.—10 to 30 per cent— dearer than molasses, except at seasons when a high demand and a total scarcity of West India rum allowed the sellers to profiteer. Occasionally, for some months together as in the summer of 1740, New England rum was quoted at exactly the same price as molasses. The margin being so small, one wonders what it was made of—and, indeed, it had no very good reputation. The rum of Pennsylvania and New York must have been a shade better: it usually (though not always) commanded 2d. or 3d. more per gallon, and John van Cortlandt spoke, in 1765, of the superiority of 'perticular New York distiled rum' over 'New England or Jew rum'.[1] But even this was much nearer, in price and in quality, to the New England rum than to the West India article.

[1] John van Cortlandt to Robert Tucker, 11 July 1765, John van Cortlandt Letter-Book, N.Y.P.L.

Various types of business were to be found in the distillery trade and, no doubt, they shaded off into each other.[1] Some distillers, at least sometimes, distilled on their own account: probably this is why we hear of their keeping out of the market for molasses because they would 'rather be idle than pay above 21d or 22'.[2] Whether there were any who never did business on any other terms, we cannot be sure. We hear of their refusing to distill by contract for others on certain occasions;[3] but those may have been occasions when the market for rum was particularly good, so that anybody with a distillery of his own would naturally insist upon taking an entrepreneur's profits. There are, on the other hand, many evidences of distilling by contract, as well as some cases of distillers who worked partly for their own account and partly for that of others. One of these intermediate cases can be seen in the complaint of the Browns of Providence: 'Mr. Nightingail has sold one hhd this week for money which we tell him is conterary to our expectations as he knew you was waits for it';[4] another, perhaps, in a letter of Messrs. Greenleaf of Boston, who hoped to obtain rum from some distillers who were in debt to them for molasses (presumably these distillers were working on their own account) 'but on requesting it found that they had contracted to deliver such quantitys of rum that they could not supply us on any terms'.[5]

The contracts usually took one of two forms: either the distiller received molasses at a certain valuation and delivered rum at a certain valuation, or he delivered the rum which came from a particular parcel of molasses and took a payment of so much per gallon for distilling. (Sometimes this payment was

[1] For an account of the geographical extension of the distillery trade, *v. supra*, pp. 32–5.

[2] S. and J. Smith, Philadelphia, to John Soley, 21 January 1768, Letter-Book of S. and J. Smith, Library of Congress. See also a letter of T. G. Steele, Newport, to Nicholas Brown and Co., 6 July 1774, Brown MSS., J.C.B.L.: 'Our distillers, . . . all decline purchasing at present as they think melasses will fall.'

[3] 'Our distillery will not distill for anybody but themselves' (William Lux, Baltimore, to Edward Rutland, 23 February 1765, Letter-Book of William Lux, N.Y.H.S.).

[4] Nicholas Brown and Co. to Benjamin Mason, 24 June 1768, Brown MSS., J.C.B.L.

[5] S. and W. Greenleaf, Boston, to Timothy Orne, 20 October 1752, Timothy Orne MSS., xi, 24, Essex Institute.

made in molasses, which is rather confusing: but it might be made in other goods, such as spermaceti candles, or in cash.)

The former kind of contract, which was, on the whole, somewhat commoner, assumed that a gallon of molasses would yield a gallon of rum. Evidently there were distillers who exacted this of their foremen, for John Browne of Newport, giving evidence in 1729 as to his contract of employment, recounted a conversation in which his employer, Captain Malbone, had said 'he did not desire me to obligate myself to make a gallon of rum for every gallon of molasses as my brother Joseph had done'.[1] Such rum must have been very bad; indeed, it was not good enough for the Royal Navy who, to the great indignation of their former supplier, began in 1768 to distill their own rum, at the rate of *two* gallons of molasses to one of rum.[2] The ratio of one to one assumed, of course, that the molasses was up to standard; where it was not, allowances had to be made, though the fairest method of dealing with inferior molasses was to have it distilled by itself for the rum it would make. But since the quality of molasses did not often vary noticeably, these exchanges of the one article into the other usually took place on a large scale quite amicably. Thus, in the course of 1758, Timothy Orne of Salem delivered over £8,000 worth (Old Tenor) of molasses at 15s. per gallon to the distiller Benjamin Hall, and received from him rum at 17s. to almost the same amount; in 1763 he delivered £4,868 (O.T.) in molasses at 11s. and 12s., receiving back £2,736 in cash and the rest in rum at 13s. 6d. and 14s. 6d.

These were the main lines on which the distillery business was conducted; but there was every possible combination and variation. The Browns' distillery at Providence, Rhode Island, turning out not more than a hogshead of rum a week, did everything by turns. The partners bought some molasses for it, and turned into it the produce of their own West India voyages, selling the rum sometimes severally, at other times in partnership. They distilled both on their own account and by contract for others. When they contracted, it was sometimes at a fixed

[1] *R.I.H.S. Magazine*, xi, 8.
[2] J. Powell, Boston, to Christopher Champlin, Newport, 19 December 1768, *Letters of Boston Merchants, 1732–1766*, Boston Public Library, MSS. I, i, 2, 83.

charge for distilling, at other times to deliver rum at a certain price and 'to have molass 1 month hence at the mean price between markett & cash'. When they distilled bad molasses, it was sometimes at an agreed deduction, at other times 'to return the rum it makes'. Besides their wholesale business they sold rum by retail.

The sugar-refining industry was not conducted in exactly the same way as the distillery. For one thing, nobody seems to have refined on contract—probably because raw sugar was not a standard article like molasses. No refiner could have undertaken to produce so much refined sugar from so much raw sugar, even if he had personally inspected the latter—much less if he had not done so. Thus, although John Watts of New York once undertook to 'convert' Havana powder sugar at 9½d. per lb. into single refined sugar at 14d. 'by way of swap . . . the refiners being fond of keeping the kettle boiling without advancing the ready mammon',[1] this was a clear case of barter; and it is significant that a Newport refiner, though sometimes ready to exchange refined sugar for brown, preferred at other times to barter it for candles: these were branded goods and he knew their quality, but the brown sugar he must at least see for himself.[2] Although there was little or no refining by contract, a merchant could obtain some claim upon a refiner's services by advancing him money or raw sugars, just as he could obtain a claim upon those of a distiller by advancing him money or molasses. But neither in the one case nor in the other was the claim a very effective one: Peter Faneuil once lamented to a correspondent, 'I had the promise of a parcell of sugar to balance your acc^t & when I came to call on the sugar baker that had promist it to me he now tells me that he cannot let me have any notwithstanding I left 300£ in his hand purely to secure the quantity you desired & now it is not to be got from any of them for money their being so great a demand for it.'[3]

Sugar-refineries, like distilleries, worked intermittently: the

[1] J.W. to John Riddell, 10 November 1763, *Letter Book of John Watts*, p. 193.

[2] John Overing, Newport, to Nicholas Brown and Co., 25 September, 28 October 1771, Brown MSS., J.C.B.L.

[3] P.F. to William Marsters, 19 September 1738, Letter-Book of Peter Faneuil, N.E.H. and G.S.

overhead costs were so slight that it was not worth while to refine except when the price of raw sugar was attractive.[1] John van Cortlandt of New York had, by his own account, quite a small sugar-house, with one pan which clarified 3,000 lb. weight, though he claimed to be able to turn out any kind of refined sugar.[2] Perhaps for this reason, he was able to keep going when other refineries in the town had to stop working because the profit margin between the price of raw sugars and the selling price of refined became too narrow.[3] Perhaps, also, since he had his own ships trading to the West Indies, he had his raw materials on more advantageous terms than those who bought in the New York market. The combination of importing and processing West India produce was, however, not very common. Most people were content with the risks and the profits of the former alone.

[1] The English sugar-refiners liked keeping their furnaces constantly in work: the heat helped to maintain the condition of their stocks of sugar already made. Perhaps the American refiners did not carry large enough stocks to make this worth while.

[2] J. van C. to Robert Tucker, 3 October 1762; to Christopher Jacobson, 21 November 1763, Letter-Book of John van Cortlandt, N.Y.P.L.

[3] J. van C. to Robert Tucker, 11 July 1765, 20 March 1766; to J. W. Hoffman, 25 September 1765, 11 January 1766. Other refiners worked intermittently according to the supplies or prices of raw sugars: for example, George Gibbs of Newport (see his letter of 24 August 1774 to the Browns, Brown MSS., J.C.B.L.).

CHAPTER IV

THE WEST INDIA TRADE IN THE NORTH AMERICAN ECONOMY

I. PROFIT AND LOSS

THE course of the trade between the northern colonies and the sugar islands has been followed from the dispatch of the outward cargo through its sale and the purchase of the returns to their arrival and disposal at the home port. Two things now remain to do: to estimate the profitableness of the trade and to show the part it played in the whole economy of North America.

To discover the profits and losses in the trade is one of the hardest things of all. There is no lack of general statements, most of them based on particular successes or, more likely, failures. But even these, for the most part, only apply to certain phases of the trade, not to the whole: in particular, they apply to the sale of the outward cargoes in the West Indies, but tell us nothing of the return cargoes, whose profits or losses may have wiped out any failure or success in the first half of the voyage. John Reynell of Philadelphia put the matter generally: 'Sometimes our goods fetch 20 [i.e. 20 per cent above cost price] sometimes 15 sometimes 10 sometimes 5 sometimes the same & sometimes less then it costs here I mean clear of all charges therefore the advantage of that trade very much depends on the timeing the remittances.'[1] Unfortunately we know least of all about the financial success of the return voyages. The owners of ships and goods received plenty of reports from their agents in the West Indies; they seldom had to render any account of their own sales, nor (which is strange) did they often trouble to calculate for their own satisfaction the profit or loss of a particular voyage or consignment.

[1] J.R. to M. L. Dicker, 19 June 1731, Reynell Letter-Book, A, p. 25, H.S.P.

SLOOP

	£	s.	d.
To the Cost of the Sloop Outsetts and Cargo—first Voyage	12,209	14	0
To Sundrys Bought in the Mount Christy and St. Croix	7,394	9	0
To Bill of Disburstments at the Mount Christy and St Croix	1,012	12	0
To Outsetts of the Vessell and Cargo 2ᵈ Voyage ..	7,949	0	0
	£28,565	15	0
To Ballance of above	11,111	13	0
To Outsett set of the Vessel and Cargo 3ᵈ Voyage ..	9,849	5	0
To Sundry Disburstments at Surinam, 2ᵈ voyage ..	1,086	16	0
To ditto	32	5	0
To 63 Hhds molasses Shipᵈ on board of the Vessel at Suriname	2,580	13	8
To Sundry Cordage Ossenbrick & Sail duck and Glass	2,730	16	2
	£27,391	8	10
To Ballance of the above	12,789	14	0
To 42 hhds mollˢ shipd on board at Suriname 2ᵈ Voyage	1,723	16	0
To Sundry Cordage on Board	2,928	10	0
To Sundry Sail dock	2,748	0	0
To Sundry disburstments 3ᵈ voyage	1,578	9	10
To 7 hhds sugar at 85 g hollᵈˢ	714	0	0
To Cash paid for 1 shott	18	0	0

(These accounts are kept
in Surinam Guilders)

£22,440 9 10

A few, however, took this trouble, at least to some degree. Perhaps it is not surprising that they stated their losses more often than their profits: for very few people feel the need to calculate or explain where all seems to be going well. Isaac Norris explained to a correspondent in 1704 that 'with striving to get West India goods' in order to obtain bills of exchange at Philadelphia upon London 'I'v strained for more than I should and lost above a thousand pounds in that trade since this time

RESOLUTION, 1766

	£	s.	d.
By Sales of the Cargo at the Mound Christy ..	8,406	7	8
By Sales of the Retorns at Providence first voyage ..	9,047	15	0
By Ballance to Ab: Whipple	11,111	13	0
	£28,565	15	0
By Sales of the Retorns at Providence 2ᵈ voyage ..	8,217	5	0
By Sales of the Cargo at Suriname 2ᵈ voyage ..	6,444	9	10
By Ballance	12,729	14	0
	27,391	8	10
By Sales of the Cargo at Suriname 2ᵈ Voyage ..	6,476	6	0
By Cash Recᵈ of de Hooy for the Voyage at Bram Point	1,296	0	0
B. W. Kennedy for freet of 4 Negroes	84	0	0
By Pork Sold	135	6	0
By One Negro sold to Abᵐ Whipple	400	0	0
By Sales of Empty hhs.	102	0	0
By 54ˡⁱ fresh Pork sold by Wolf	10	8	0
By Ballance or Cost of the vessell and Cargo ..	13,936	9	10
	£22,440	9	10

12 ᵐᵒ [twelvemonth].'[1] Since we do not know the scale of his enterprises, this tells us little; perhaps we should attach more importance to his statement that he expected to recover only 60 per cent of the corn he had sent to the West Indies.[2] But this was only an estimate or prophecy.

The ledger of Peter Faneuil of Boston gives us more reliable

---

[1] I.N. to John Askew, 8 December 1704, Isaac Norris Letter-Book, iii, 10, H.S.P.
[2] I.N. to Joseph Pike, 18 February 1709/10, *ibid.*, v, 134.

detail; but, unfortunately for our purpose, he usually acted as factor for Frenchmen in the West Indies, and his own ventures, on which alone he estimated the profit and loss, were very few. A small venture to Martinique at the end of 1728 seems to have yielded him a high rate of profit: it cost him £54 10s. 0d. and the return cargo sold for £141 3s. 6d.—profit, £86 13s. 6d. A voyage to St. Eustatius in 1730, on the other hand, made a loss of £146 15s. 7d. on an outlay of £600 3s. 4d., chiefly because part of the cargo proved unsaleable. These were the only West India ventures on his own account, though he occasionally speculated by buying part of the cargoes consigned to him by his correspondents and sending rum or molasses up or down the coast: these speculations were nearly always successful.[1] He gives one more estimate in a letter: a cargo costing less than £700 earned a profit of between £400 and £500, the returns being mostly molasses and rum: but since he refers to 'a six weeks voyage' it is almost certain that the destination was not the West Indies but Louisbourg, from which outpost French West India produce was occasionally imported into Boston.[2]

Two other calculations come from the papers of the Brown family. One of them concerns the Sloop *Resolution*, and I print it entire.[3] It is kept, for some reason, in Surinam guilders. Although it does not distinguish the value of the sloop from that of the first cargo, nor does it at any subsequent point distinguish the cargo from the 'outset'—i.e. the ship's stores, repairs, etc.— it gives some idea of the exchange of cargoes between North America and the West Indies, at any rate from half-way through the first voyage to half-way through the third, and of the relative weight of the disbursements in the islands.

The second calculation, which I print also, is more explicit, though summary.

OCT 18 1773. Memo[dm] About M Jos & Moses Brown's Loss Since there present Comp[y] w[ch] began in the Spring 1771 Note they have not got anything in any one Voyage Since Capt Chris[r] Sheldon & Simons Arrival from Surinam in the summer 1771

---

[1] Ledger of Peter Faneuil, ff. 176, 226, 242, 325 (N.E.H. and G.S.).
[2] P.F. to Peter Warren, 19 September 1737, Letter-Book of Peter Faneuil, *ibid.*
[3] Pp. 140–1.

Note the old Brigt Geo: was Val^d when Divided at 1,000 Dol^{rs} as she Came from Sea. she has made 3 very bad Voyages & run out so as to be sunk & worth nothing of any Value

	Lmy
1st Voyage by Chris^r Whipple Lost	£155
2^d Voyage, by Capt Gregory Lost	190
3^d Voyage, by do	198
Sloop Betsy to Virginia	120
Sloop A, Bradford	105
Suppose We have in protested Dutch bills Unsertain— by Calculation	£1,333
[debts in Virginia & London etc.]	
Protested Dutch bills bad & Good for nothing	150
. . . Lost last year—the same Vessels	350
. . . Lost in the year before	240
Lost on Dutch Bills sent to Turner p̄ his letter lately rec^d	157

It may be assumed that the three voyages of the Brigantine *George* were to Surinam; that of the Sloop "A" was to the French West Indies; the Dutch bills of exchange were undoubtedly obtained as payment for northern produce sold at Surinam. Only the voyage of the *Betsey* to Virginia, and the bad debts owing from that colony, are irrelevant to our purpose. We do not know the values of the cargoes upon which these losses were made, except that of the Sloop "A", which was £651 lawful money. Those of the Brigantine *George* may be conjectured to be about £1,200 each, and to each voyage there must be added, say, £120 for wages and something—say £200, though an estimate is almost impossible—for repairs and other disbursements on the ship at the home port. These figures, if they mean anything, show that for the four West India voyages, on an average capital of about £1,400 there was an average loss of £162, without any allowance for depreciation of shipping.

Of course West India voyages did not always lose at this rate; it was just because such losses were exceptional that the Browns made a memorandum of them. Their earlier voyages were much more satisfactory: and their papers provide, perhaps, the best opportunity we have of estimating, however imperfectly, the profit or loss of a West India voyage.

The Sloop *George*, Abraham Whipple, master, cleared from Providence for Surinam on 12 February 1763. The sloop herself was valued 'supposed to be when come hoome' at £9,000 Old Tenor currency. (The rate of conversion from Old Tenor to Lawful Money in that year was 23⅓ to 1.) There was a charge of £3,197 10s. od. for 'goods for the vessel's use'—largely provisions for the crew—and the cost of graving the ship, sails, loading the cargo, etc., came to £4,843. The cargo was worth £23,314 7s. 3d., so the whole outfit came to £40,254 17s. 3d. In addition, the portledge bill—the wages of the officers and crew—came to £2,998. The cargo sold at Surinam for 12,747 guilders, local currency. The port charges amounted to 1,278 guilders, other disbursements to 927 guilders. This left 10,542 guilders available for buying the return cargo. Of this sum, 6,516 guilders were laid out in 20,050 gallons of molasses, 600 guilders in two Negro boys; 800 guilders were due to the captain for his commission of 5 per cent on sales and 2½ per cent on returns. This would leave 2,626 guilders to be invested in bills of exchange on Holland. We do not know what bills were bought; but supposing the whole sum to have been invested in a bill, at the rate of 6 Surinam guilders to 5 Hollands guilders, it would amount to 2,188 Hollands guilders or about £191 sterling (nearly £4,400 Old Tenor). The molasses sold in Rhode Island for 40s. per gallon. We do not know if there was any wastage; but if we assume 5 per cent, the value would be about £38,000. The value of the Negro boys is unknown—probably they were wanted for domestic service; but even if they had both died and the bills of exchange had all been protested without any chance of recovery (which is most unlikely) the molasses alone would have paid all the other expenses and nearly half the value of the sloop. This may be called a successful voyage.

In September 1764 the Brig *George*—a different vessel under the same Captain Whipple—set sail likewise for Surinam. The vessel was valued at £9,000, the rigging, etc., £5,000, the cargo and crew's provisions £26,749 11s. od. The total outset, including 5 per cent commission on the cargo and provisions (presumably paid to the captain in advance for selling the cargo), and a month's advance of pay to the crew, was

£42,599 5s. 11d. The portledge bill amounted to about £4,800. The cargo sold for 12,871 Surinam guilders; the port charges were 1,122 guilders and the other disbursements 835 guilders. 19,708 gallons of molasses were bought for 6,405 guilders, and a bill of exchange bought for 1,593 guilders = 1,327 Hollands guilders = £116 sterling, or about £2,500 Old Tenor. This leaves 2,754 guilders unaccounted for (after the captain's 2½ per cent on sales is deducted): perhaps it was left behind to be invested in another bill of exchange or in molasses to be remitted by another of the Browns' vessels. The *George* reached Providence with 18,350 gallons of molasses. Unfortunately we do not know the price of sale. Supposing it to have been 36s. per gallon, the bill of exchange to have been paid and the money unaccounted for not to have been thrown away, this was another successful voyage.[1]

No other voyage, even of the Browns, is so fully documented: sometimes essential figures are missing, often the concerns of different voyages were mingled together, for the Browns often had two or three vessels at a time in the river of Surinam, the senior captain managing all of them and remitting the proceeds of their cargoes indiscriminately. But enough has been said to show that a West India voyage could be extremely profitable. Probably the Surinam trade was more profitable than most, because molasses abounded and the port charges were relatively low. But even the Surinam trade did not always yield success, as the jeremiad of 1773, already quoted, has shown.

The voyages just described illustrate the value of the trade to those who owned their own shipping, which most merchants did who had extensive dealings with the West Indies. Different documents, scattered and fragmentary, show the charges in-

[1] The price at which this molasses sold has to be guessed; 36 shillings per gallon seems a reasonable conclusion from the following facts. The earlier cargo was disposed of about the middle of 1763, at 40 shillings per gallon. Although I have not any statistics of molasses prices in Rhode Island for this period, some inferences can be drawn from the prices at Boston and New York. In the first part of 1765 when the second cargo must have been sold, the New York price was almost the same as in the middle of 1763, and the Boston price was 20 per cent lower than it had been. If the Rhode Island price was a mean between those of Boston and New York (which is quite likely, considering its geographical situation) it would work out about 36 shillings.

curred by those who took freight upon the ships of others; but hardly one shows us the whole transaction from beginning to end. Indeed, the only impression we can get is that of the very heavy cost of freight and of having goods sold on commission. For instance, 16 hogsheads of molasses sent from St. Kitts to Philadelphia in 1723 yielded £88 7s. 8d. gross, but only £57 1s. 8d. remained after duty, freight, cooperage, commission, etc., had been paid. In return, flour, bacon and bread to the value of £51 3s. 8d. was bought but only £42 0s. 3d. represented the prime cost.[1] We are not to say this venture was not profitable, for we do not know what the rum cost or the flour fetched at St. Kitts; but we know that the cost of transport and distribution were high in proportion to the value of the goods—for in this case they were nearly 50 per cent on the whole transaction, without reckoning the $4\frac{1}{2}$ per cent export duty on the molasses or the freight of the flour, both of which were paid in St. Kitts.

II. THE INCIDENTAL USES OF THE WEST INDIA TRADE

Much as the profits of this trade must have contributed to the formation of capital, this was not the only part which it played in North American economy. Above all, it facilitated the payment of debts to Europe, and so lubricated the trans-Atlantic trade. This was particularly true at the beginning of colonial history, when the flow of capital to the West must have been relatively heavy and the means of making a direct payment in return had not yet been developed. It was equally true of every succeeding new colony—Philadelphia about 1700 was in the same position as Boston about 1650—and of new merchants in old-established colonies: for a beginner without the necessary connections or expertise was more likely than an old hand to rely on 'returns *via* the West Indies'. Even old colonies, and well-established merchants, who traded no longer as mere agents of Englishmen but on their own account, found the West India trade, and the trade in West India goods, a

---

[1] Wooddrop Account Book, Library of Congress, Ac. 741. It will be observed that this transaction is unusual, for the adventurer was a West Indian and the Philadelphia merchant sold on commission.

very useful, indeed necessary, device for settling the balance of payments between North America and Europe.

There were more ways than one of doing this. The crudest, though in some respects the safest, was to bring the West India produce to a North American port and forward it from thence to Europe on any ship that offered. This had the advantage that the timing and the security of the remittance did not depend upon the energy or the good faith of a West Indian agent—a consideration which might well outweigh the additional risk and expense of a double voyage. Accordingly, in 1648 and 1650, we find business men in Boston shipping indigo, a West Indian product, to London,[1] and in 1662, 1663 and 1665 vessels bringing sugar from Boston to London.[2] In May 1666 Peleg Sanford of Newport, Rhode Island, desires his cousin living in Boston 'that if any shipping arives from London, and tht the prices of sug^r should arise to 20s. or 22s. per hundred y^t you would sell sume of myne y^t lyes in yor storehouses'.[3]

1763

This trade was deliberately knocked on the head by the Plantation Act of 1673, which imposed a duty on West India produce exported to North America, and so made it too expensive to re-export to England where it paid duty again. Only certain eccentric or transitory substitutes survived. Merchants in Liverpool, and later others in Newburyport, Massachusetts, occasionally arranged for consignments of New England rum to that smugglers' paradise, the Isle of Man, where the Liverpool slave-traders were in the habit of filling up with cheap rum— all the cheaper for having paid no duty on arrival—for their voyages to the African coast. In Ireland, too, there seem to have been places where rum could be landed without much risk of paying duty.[4] But the North American merchants did not often find it worth while to re-export fairly and

---

[1] *Aspinwall Notarial Records*, pp. 409, 418. On p. 292 is the record of a slightly different transaction: thirty rolls of Barbados tobacco are shipped from Charlestown on a Dutch ship to Madeira, presumably to pay a debt for wine.

[2] *Suffolk Deeds*, iv, 49, 226; v, 72.

[3] P.S. to Elisha Hutchinson, *Letter-Book of Peleg Sanford*, p. 8.

[4] Harris and Cuming to James Hudson, 4 February 1752, Hudson-Rogers Papers, Box i, N.Y.P.L.; M. and T. Dalton, Newbury, to Hudson, 29 January 1762, *ibid.*

squarely.[1] New England rum, perhaps, was not open to the same objection; for it had not originated in the West Indies, and its raw material, molasses, which had done so had almost certainly been imported into North America without paying more than a nominal duty. But New England rum was not likely to find an extensive market in Great Britain, in competition with the better West India article as well as malt spirits.

The one great exception to these generalizations took place in war-time. Since the North Americans traded so freely with the enemy's sugar colonies, and since the enemy himself was under such difficulties in bringing home his colonial produce to Europe, what could be more natural than the rise of a re-export trade in French sugars from New England and New York to Hamburg, Amsterdam, Cadiz, Gibraltar, Leghorn and even London—to say nothing of the prize sugars of which such quantities were brought in as the local markets could never absorb? An owner of privateers like Philip Cuyler of New York would necessarily have prize sugars to dispose of, if his men had any luck.[2] So too would a persistent trader with the enemy like Richard Derby of Salem: captains in the employ of this family were at Valencia, Gibraltar and possibly Leghorn in the Seven Years War, and they did not all take the trouble to come home to Salem before making for Europe: often they proceeded straight from Monte Cristi or from the enemy's ports.[3]

Besides these traders whose ventures in French sugars to Europe were almost a necessary consequence of their other business, there was a whole host of speculators, especially at New York: the rumour of their business reached as far north as

[1] There were exceptions: Edmund Quincey junior of Boston instructed Captain Robert Sinclair to sell both New England and West India rum in Leith, where there can have been little hope of evading duties, and remit the proceeds in a bill of exchange to Rotterdam (see his letter of 14 April 1745, among the papers of the *Providence*, Public Record Office, High Court of Admiralty Miscellanea, 663).

[2] P.C. to John Hodshon, Amsterdam, 17 January 1758, Letter-Book of Philip Cuyler, N.Y.P.L. Cuyler also had a share in a flag-of-truce vessel, which probably brought him in French sugars in quite a different way. (See his letter to his father, 3 December 1759, *ibid.*)

[3] Orders to Captain John Brown, 8 April 1759, Derby Family MSS., vol. xxiii, Essex Institute; Richard Derby, Jr., to Richard Derby, Sr., 4 March 1760, *ibid.*, vol. xxiv; George Crowninshield, Gibraltar, to Richard Derby, 22 December 1759, *ibid.*, vol. xii; Anderson and Macniel, Gibraltar, 6 August 1760, 30 September 1761, *ibid.*

Portsmouth, New Hampshire, where they chartered three ships and a snow, and inspired the local ship-owners with hopes of similar charters at other ports.[1] Some of these speculators were content, like G. G. Beekman, to ship to Europe such West India produce as they could command from their own resources.[2] Others, such as Waddell Cunningham, wanted to buy sugars with bills drawn on London merchants; they therefore found 'a great want, that we have not a house fix'd in London that we can depend upon, to answer our bills when we have to make purchases, that has a prospect to answer at that market, Holland or Hamburgh'.[3] This was a highly risky business, for it depended not only on the fluctuations of trade but also on war, politics and even law: a decision of the Lords Commissioners of Prize Appeals in London might at any moment flood the European markets by releasing sugars which had remained for months locked up in law-suits.[4] Even without such accidents the trade was overdone: 'Rum', wrote a firm of Gibraltar merchants to Richard Derby, 'continues to be a perfect drugg in this garrison, there being at present in it a sufficiency for its consumption for nigh two years.'[5] Yet the trade must have had its profits, and one or two outlets for West India produce and for New England enterprise must have been permanently opened by this war. Timothy Orne, indeed, made nothing of a venture in cocoa, sugar and rum to Cadiz in 1763: the cocoa was bad, there was no demand for the sugar and rum. But Gibraltar was a British garrison town, and the demand for rum, whether West India or New England, was still brisk in 1766 and 1767.[6]

[1] John Sherburne, Portsmouth, N.H., to John Reynell, 15 March 1760, Coates-Reynell Papers, Box xi, H.S.P.

[2] G. G. Beekman to A. Schoales, 9 September 1760, Letter-Book of G. G. Beekman, N.Y.H.S.

[3] Greg and Cunningham to W. Snell and Co., London, 4 June 1756, Letter-Book of Greg and Cunningham, N.Y.H.S., p. 43; Waddell Cunningham to T. Greg, 11 December 1756, *ibid.*, p. 200.

[4] According to Messrs. Anderson and Macniel, of Gibraltar, the decision against some Monte Cristi vessels in the summer of 1760, followed by public sales of the condemned sugars, lowered prices at Gibraltar (see their letters of 6 and 21 August 1760 to Richard Derby, in Derby Family MSS., vol. xii, Essex Institute).

[5] The same to Richard Derby, 30 September 1761, *ibid.*

[6] Robert Anderson and Co., Gibraltar, to Richard Derby, 29 March 1766, 7 October 1767, *ibid.*

⸤Bringing West India goods to North America and sending them on to Europe can never have been the most profitable traffic, except at certain emergencies. This was not only a matter of the Plantation Duties, or even of the double freight and risk. It was common sense and it saved time to consign West India produce straight from the islands in payment of North American debts.⸥ This too began very early. In the first transactions of all, the Londoners probably arranged the transactions on their own account, perhaps as the best way of provisioning sugar or tobacco plantations in which they were financially interested: for instance, in 1651 three London merchants freighted the *John and Sara* to proceed to Charlestown in New England, there to deliver servants to their agent, who was to sell them and load the vessel for Barbados with provisions which another agent would sell, returning the proceeds to London.[1] But venturers were more often, even at first, North Americans.[2] Even the colony of Rhode Island, having a debt to repay to their agent in London, levied goods to be sold in Barbados for the purpose: provisions were preferred to horses, a more speculative article, for this consignment, since the colony being a corporation of agriculturalists and not a merchant entrepreneur, wanted above all to be sure of paying the debt.[3]

Business men continued for several generations to consign ventures upon their own account to the West Indies in order to put money into their London correspondents' pockets by having the proceeds remitted to them in sugar and rum. Samuel Sewall did so via Antigua;[4] Isaac Norris via Nevis, Barbados and Jamaica.[5]

It was, at best, a clumsy business to send goods to the West Indies and thence forward other goods to London. As time

---

[1] *Suffolk Deeds*, i, 5.

[2] For example, *Suffolk Deeds*, iv, 35; viii, 31. The payment of debts already contracted is not easily distinguished from the negotiation of loans upon bottomry (*ibid.*, i, 261; *Essex County, Records and Files of the Quarterly Court*, ii, 124).

[3] *R.I. Col. Rec.*, i, 444, 482–3; *Early Records of the Town of Providence*, xv, 91.

[4] S.S. to Nathaniel Barns, 26 October 1688, *Letter Books of Samuel Sewall*, i, 84.

[5] I.N. to J. Pinnell, 29 July 1699, Letter-Books of Isaac Norris, i, 35, H.S.P.; I.N. to John Askew, 29 October 1702, *ibid.*, ii, 2; I.N. to Abel Bond, 5 November 1702, *ibid.*, ii, 3; I.N. to H. Coward and W. Suttle, 22 November 1708, *ibid.*, iv, 216.

went on and the colonial trade became specialized, the creditors and correspondents of North Americans became less and less qualified to handle consignments of West India produce and less and less willing to receive them. A northern merchant who shipped such produce to England on his own account was liable to make costly mistakes in the choice of a factor to sell it. Moreover, a sugar-factor in the eighteenth century, however willing to advance thousands for a sugar-planter, would not care to give credit even for hundreds to a mere merchant, without any mortgageable property, in a colony of which he knew nothing.[1] Peleg Sanford of Rhode Island did indeed find such a correspondent in 1666; but that correspondent seems to have 'abused' him,[2] and I doubt if he could have found one at all seventy years later. Moreover, there was no need to do business in this way at all. When every planter became anchored, so to speak, to his own sugar-factor, drawing bills of exchange for every payment, nothing, it seemed, should have been easier for a North American with fish or bread or lumber to sell, or already sold, than to buy such bills in the islands.

From the first foundation of the colonies, bills of exchange were a common means of remittance. But in the early days, before the colonies which retained some degree of financial dependence had differentiated themselves from those which depended absolutely upon the mother-country, this traffic in bills of exchange flowed in more than one direction, even within the same channel. Thus we find merchants in New England drawing bills, for moneys due to them, on merchants in Barbados; these bills might be made payable in London or paid on the spot in sugar which could be remitted to London. We also find the agents of London merchants drawing bills in New England on their principals, and New Englanders who possessed credits in London drawing their own bills in payment for West India goods.[3] All this was exceptional in the eighteenth century. A few British merchants, like John Reynell's early correspondents in the west of England, still sent their

---

[1] See my book, *A West India Fortune*, pp. 240–2.

[2] P.S. to Wm. Pate, 7 December 1666, 18 December 1667; to Wm. Sanford, 28 December 1668, *Letter Book of Peleg Sanford*, pp. 15, 38, 69.

[3] *Aspinwall Notarial Records*, pp. 292, 356; *Suffolk Deeds*, vii, 283.

ships to North America to take in lumber for the West Indies and empowered their captains to draw bills upon them for the purpose; but there were not many examples of this.[1] The merchants of the commercial colonies in North America were not often in a position to draw bills on England, especially for an article like West India produce which they could so easily earn by the sale of their own goods. So far from laying out cash or bills for this purpose, they were more concerned to obtain bills from their neighbours the tobacco-planters (who got credits in Europe by the sale of their weed) by peddling West India produce among them.[2]

There were two classes of exceptions; and they can both be explained. In the early years of Philadelphia we hear of merchants sending bills on London to the West Indies in order to buy sugar and rum, or earning bills on London by the sale of sugar and rum in Philadelphia itself.[3] But, as I have observed already, Philadelphia before 1700 was in the same financial position as Boston about 1650; the colony was still drawing on English resources and the merchants were more intimately connected with those of London and Bristol than they were later. Like causes produced like results. The other exception was common in the Seven Years War. Speculators, especially in New York, not content with buying up prize goods for shipment to Europe, sometimes offered to give bills for cargoes of sugar and rum straight from the West Indies.[4] This could never have happened without a number of unusual circumstances: the artificial derangement of the transit of sugar between the French West Indies and France, the opening of new markets in Europe, the heavy military expenditure in North America which rendered bills plentiful and rum a winning speculation.

[1] Michael Atkins, Bristol, to John Reynell, 30 June 1737, Coates-Reynell Papers, Box ii, H.S.P.; M. L. Dicker, Exeter, to J.R., 3 February 1752, *ibid.*, Box vii.

[2] Isaac Norris to John Askew, 9 July 1703, Letter-Books of Isaac Norris, ii, 68, H.S.P.; Jonathan Dickinson to John Hotchkins, 30 September 1720, Letter-Book of Jonathan Dickinson, p. 360, L.C.P.

[3] Isaac Norris to Abel Bond, 5 November 1702, Letter-Books of Isaac Norris, ii, 2, H.S.P.; to John Askew, 8 December 1704, *ibid.*, iii, 10.

[4] Greg and Cunningham, New York, to William Woodbridge, 4 July 1756, Letter-Book of Greg and Cunningham, N.Y.H.S.; John Watts to Gedney Clarke, 23 July 1765, *Letter-Book of John Watts*, p. 361.

With these exceptions, the trade, during the eighteenth
century, all flowed in the same channel: the North Americans
sold their produce in the sugar islands and, if they wanted a
remittance to Europe, bought the planters' bills of exchange on
their factors.

This sounds simple; but in fact there were many difficulties
and pitfalls. It was not always easy to buy bills at all, especially
when the crop of a particular island was short and the soberer
planters doubted whether they would have any balances upon
which to draw.[1] When the supply of bills was thus affected, the
premium of exchange might rise so high that they became unprofitable to buy; several North American captains shipped
money rather than take bills at an excessive rate.[2] More
serious still was the danger of bad bills. The real state of a
planter's finances was a very difficult thing to find out, indeed
very few planters seem to have known it themselves. They were
too sanguine, and too apt, at the very least, to draw bills on the
strength of sugars which they found themselves, in the end,
unable to make or obliged to devote to some other use.[3] Even
the merchants resident in the islands made mistakes in accepting bills, and it is hard to see how transient captains can have
known what they were about, even if, like the Browns' captains
at Surinam, they frequented the same colony again and again.

There was, of course, a remedy when bills were protested for
non-payment: the laws of each colony allowed damages to be
claimed at a fixed rate. But this did not really compensate for
all the bother and delay, especially as the rate of damages fixed
in some of the sugar colonies was rather low. This constituted
a special danger for those North Americans who, instead of
sending the bills they had bought to Europe on their own
account, sold them for ready money in North America, where
the damages on protested bills (to which endorsers as well as
drawers were liable) were higher than in the West Indies.[4]
This they might well wish to do, either because they needed the

[1] Henry Bonnin, Antigua, to Reynell and Rabley, 15 February 1730/1, Coates-
Reynell Papers, Box i, H.S.P.; to John Reynell, 9 April 1731, *ibid.*

[2] Henry Bonnin to John Reynell, 16 May 1733, *ibid.*

[3] William Dunbar, Antigua, to John Reynell, 27 January 1755, *ibid.*, Box
ix.

[4] David Fogo, Antigua, to John Reynell, 29 August 1754, *ibid.*, Box viii.

money for a purchase at home (as the Browns needed it to buy head-matter for their spermaceti candle manufactory),[1] or because they did not know how else to get in the money.

Dutch bills, brought home from St. Eustatius and Surinam, were a particularly difficult problem, for the North Americans had little direct trade with Holland and little occasion to spend Dutch money. Holders could only part with Dutch bills at a heavy loss. The best way to turn them into cash was to send them to be negotiated in London and draw bills on London covered by them.[2] But this required a settled correspondent in London, and he might have to be paid for his risks; for Dutch bills were risky—much money was lost by Surinam bills in the financial crisis of 1772. Happy was the North American merchant who could induce a London financier, by paying him a premium of $2\frac{1}{2}$ per cent, to guarantee all bills, British or Dutch, remitted to him.[3]

Although remittances of goods and bills of exchange were the methods by which most North Americans used the West India trade in order to pay their debts in Great Britain, they were not the only ways. The earnings of North American shipping could be used for the same purpose. Several things must be distinguished here. Vessels were built in the North American ports to the orders of British merchants, whether for the West India trade or for some other; similar vessels were built on speculation for sale in the islands[4] or, more likely, in England; and these last might well go by way of the islands in order to add to the profit by taking a freight of sugar across the Atlantic.[5] But besides these, other ships which were not only built but wholly or partly owned in America plied as regular 'stationed ships', fixed in the trade between a particular island and Great

[1] Nicholas Brown and Co. to Capt. Nicholas Power, 30 April 1768, papers of Brig *Sally*, 1767, Brown MSS., J.C.B.L.

[2] Nicholas Brown and Co. to Hayley and Hopkins, London, 10 May 1769, 11 April 1771, *ibid.*

[3] *Ibid.*, Thomas Clifford to Thomas Franks, Bristol, 4 August 1772, Clifford Correspondence, xxviii, 290, H.S.P.

[4] Robert Ellis, Philadelphia, to Lawrence Williams, London, 14 August 1738, Letter-Book of Robert Ellis, p. 127, H.S.P.

[5] Messrs. Thomas and John Randall Phillips, Barbados, to James Hudson, 31 May 1758, Hudson-Rogers Papers, N.Y.P.L.; James Hudson to W. Rogers, 24 July 1758, *ibid.*

Britain[1] or (less frequently) in a triangular traffic between
Great Britain, North America and the West Indies.[2] They had
to be specially built for the West India trade: they must carry
nothing but hogsheads (for sugar was seldom shipped home in
smaller cask) and three tiers or 'heights' of hogsheads at that,
which necessitated two decks.[3]

This may have been a lucrative trade when sugar crops were
good, planters clamouring for ship-room, and freight rates
therefore high; but a short crop was at least as common as a
great one, and then North Americans might have to lie four or
six months for a freight, perhaps right into the hurricane season,
and even the stationed ships from London, whose 'interest' was
superior to all others, might have to repair to the ports of the
continent for a freight.[4] Moreover, there were vexations even
when the freight rates were high: several North American
owners complained that their ships 'lay by the walls' too long
in London or Bristol, at great expense in seamen's wages, for
want of proper dispatch in unloading cargo or procuring a
return freight.[5] Such negligence was by no means improbable,
for the ships would presumably be consigned to sugar-factors,
who would hardly give them the same attention as to those
owned by themselves or even by their indispensable correspondents the planters. This would apply even more to such
North American vessels as might casually take a freight of sugar
to England once in a while, for want of any other employment
in the islands.[6] They would find other difficulties too: not
having been built for a trade which consisted entirely of hogs-

[1] Benjamin Wright to Aaron Lopez, 14 March and 19 June 1773, *Commerce of
Rhode Island*, i, 433, 443.

[2] Jonathan Dickinson to Isaac Gale, 24 September 1720, Letter-Book of Jonathan Dickinson, p. 360, L.C.P.; J.D. to John Askew, 27 September, 6 December
1720, *ibid.*, pp. 354, 367; Thomas Clifford to Thomas Franks, Bristol, 16 September 1774, Clifford Correspondence, xxix, 46, H.S.P.

[3] Jonathan Dickinson to Isaac Gale, 24 September 1720, Letter-Book of Jonathan Dickinson, p. 360; Henry Bonnin, Antigua, to John Reynell, 16 May 1733,
Coates-Reynell Papers, Box i, H.S.P.

[4] Michael Lovell, Antigua, to John Reynell, 30 March 1737, 29 July 1738,
ibid., Box ii; Birkett and Booth, Antigua, to John Reynell, 9 October 1747, *ibid.*,
Box iv.

[5] John Reynell to M. L. Dicker, 15 September 1735, Reynell Letter-Book,
i, 20.

[6] Such voyages are described by Mr. Byron Fairchild, *op. cit.*, pp. 69, 115–17.

heads, they would have to waste space or to fill up with cotton and small casks on the owners' account.[1] Nevertheless, a number of North American owners and captains chose this employment for their vessels, either because they could not get molasses cheap enough to make a profitable voyage to North America,[2] or because they found a merchant in the islands who would promise them a freight of sugar to England if they would sell him their cargoes cheap enough.[3]

In spite of all disadvantages, vessels built and, in many cases, owned in North America engaged in the trade between the West Indies and Great Britain in such numbers as to nettle by their competition the owners of the regular London-built ships. These owners often warned the planters solemnly against entrusting their property to such inferior shipping. These warnings were sometimes quite sincere. Henry Lascelles owned many of the regular ships in the trade; but he seems also to have had a share in a vessel of New England origin, the *Argo*, and she carried some of the sugars from his own plantation. In 1751 he lamented her 'going ashore at Carlisle Bay in but a midling storm, which I am informed was occasioned by her bad ground Tackling—This has often been the case with Ships that come directly from New England, which are generally fitted out from thence in that villainous manner, so that I must beg you will please for your sake as well as mine, never to put any Goods on board such Ships, if Freight is to be got otherwise.'[4] This incident appears to have made an impression upon the minds of the planters, for, next year, the House of Lascelles and Maxwell wrote, 'We observe, though the Crops are far short of what was expected, there will be sufficient to load all the Ships belonging to the Trade, and that people will be very Cautious of shipping in New England Bottoms that have not been fitted in London.'

[1] John Reynell to N. Donnell, 29 March 1756, Reynell Letter-Book, iii, H.S.P.
[2] Moses Wingate, Jamaica, to John Reynell, 2 April 1761, Coates-Reynell Papers, Box xi, H.S.P.
[3] Peter Hunter to John Reynell, 7 July 1749, *ibid.*, Box vii; Samuel Sweet, St. Christophers, to Messrs. Tyler, Bowler and Champlin, 29 March 1758, Champlin Papers, R.I.H.S.
[4] This document is quoted from the papers of Messrs. Wilkinson and Gaviller, which were destroyed in the blitz of 1940, and exist, so far as I know, only in my transcripts.

It is difficult to estimate the importance of these earnings to the North American traders. Some people spoke of them as indispensable: for instance, a town meeting at Boston declared in 1736 that 'nothing saves that trade' [the West India trade] 'but the freights from thence to London'.[1] This seems to have been a great exaggeration: in the merchants' correspondence plans and half-intentions are much talked of, but actual voyages, of any kind, in this trade are exceptional.

In many other ways, too, the West India trade and the trade in West India goods played an incidental but useful part in the economy of North America. Some of this is easily discerned— for example, the exports of rum from Boston and Rhode Island[2] to the African coast, where it was bartered for Negro slaves who were later sold in the West Indies for bills of exchange on London or Bristol. No less obvious, as a means of earning money in London, were the exports of rum and molasses to Newfoundland,[3] or to the tobacco colonies,[4] where the fishermen and the planters respectively gave their bills on London in exchange for it. This last trade was a standby, not only for New England ship-owners who wanted to keep their crews together in the winter[5] but also for merchants whose ships had brought home from the islands more rum and molasses than the local market would absorb, or for sugar-refiners likewise anxious to dispose of their surplus,[6] or even to anybody who wanted to make a little money and was ready to buy West India goods for a venture to the southward.[7] It had its risks, above all that of bad debts: in the tobacco colonies, as in the sugar colonies, neither planters nor merchants excelled in prompt payments, and the ship-owners of Salem or Rhode

---

[1] Minutes of Boston Town Meeting, 1 January 1735/6, *Boston Records, 1729–42*, p. 121 (*Boston Record Commission, Report no. 12*).

[2] More than three-quarters of the rum exported from North America to Africa in 1772 came from Boston and Rhode Island.

[3] Joseph Tillinghast, St. Johns, Newfoundland, to Nicholas Brown and Co., 28 July 1771, Brown MSS., J.C.B.L.

[4] Isaac Norris to R. Poor, 13 December 1699, 5 April 1700, Isaac Norris Letter-Book, i, 117, 161, H.S.P.

[5] *V. supra*, p. 19.

[6] See the Letter-Book of John van Cortlandt, 1762–1768, N.Y.P.L., *passim*.

[7] Samuel Lee, Manchester, Mass., to Timothy Orne, 19 November 1758, Timothy Orne MSS., iii, 143, Essex Institute.

Island had to caution their masters to sell any debts outstanding at their departure to whoever would buy them up, rather than leave any behind.[1] (Indeed, this was probably one of the reasons why such vessels were more often consigned to the masters than to the merchants of Virginia and Maryland, who made fair proffers and elaborate schemes, but did not even pretend to return the value of the cargo by the vessel: sometimes they got so far behind with their payments that the owners had to send a special agent, as the Browns of Providence had to send Captain Coffin to recover their property from the plausible Messrs. Adams and Griffin of Virginia.[2]) But in spite of these risks the trade was a useful one: when it did not yield bills of exchange, it provided cargoes of farm produce and lumber which might be further used, directly or indirectly, in the West India trade, and so keep the wheels of commerce turning.[3]

Again, the West India trade itself could be used as a means of payment between one part of the continent and another: thus the merchants of Portsmouth, New Hampshire, who wanted money in Philadelphia ordered their ships thither with cargoes of rum and molasses from St. Kitts or salt from Salt Tortuga; their object was to obtain flour and bread, or to pay for flour and bread they had already received, presumably for their own consumption.[4]

The voyages just described can be explained by the need of merchants in the commercial centres to earn, however indirectly, money in Europe or by the economic diversity of North America whose regions required each other's products and exchanged them by means of West India goods. But there were interchanges between the commercial centres which can

---

[1] Timothy Orne frequently gave such instructions to his captains.

[2] Adams and Griffin, Elm Tree, Virginia, to John Brown, 28 September 1768, Brown MSS., J.C.B.L.; Nicholas Brown and Co., to Adams and Griffin, 17 April, 25 June 1771, *ibid.*

[3] John van Cortlandt of New York consigned a cargo of rum to Adams and Griffin of Virginia, in order to get a load of peas and corn for Barbados (J. van C. to Captain Depeyster, 7 February 1767, van Cortlandt Letter-Book, N.Y.P.L.). For this subject generally, see A. P. Middleton, *Tobacco Coast* (Newport News, 1953), pp. 198–9.

[4] John Sherburne, Portsmouth, N.H., to John Reynell, 17 February 1752, Coates-Reynell Papers, Box vii; same to same, 18 March 1756, *ibid.*, Box ix, H.S.P.

only be described as speculative. The purpose of these interchanges and the parties active in them cannot be defined more precisely. Whereas the commercial centres were nearly always the active parties in the trade which radiated from them to the agricultural, lumbering and fishing districts—a Philadelphian traded to Virginia, a Rhode Islander to Newfoundland, or even a New London man to Long Island[1] on his own account, not on that of his correspondents—it is hard to discern any definite current in the intercourse between the principal ports, or even between primary centres like Boston or Providence and secondary ones like Louisbourg[2] or Nantucket.[3] Certain persistent tendencies, however, can perhaps be perceived.

For one thing, the prices of sugar at Boston, New York, and Philadelphia normally varied less from each other (allowing for the several currencies) than those of molasses and rum. This is not surprising: sugar was comparatively valuable in proportion to its bulk, and could therefore be carried with comparative ease, especially between New York and Philadelphia, in order to adjust any striking differences between the prices at the respective ports. Moreover, the consumption of sugar was comparatively small, so that the quantities which would have to be carried from port to port for this purpose would not be great. Rum and, still more, molasses were bulky articles, and the consumption everywhere was great; larger quantities, therefore, than it was usually worth while to send would be needed in order to bring the different prices into line with each other. Nevertheless, there were some years, and not only in war-time, when it was clearly worth while to carry rum or molasses from Boston to Philadelphia or New York. The price of New England rum was normally a good deal lower in Boston

[1] See the *Diary of Joshua Hempstead*, pp. 67, 101, 116: on 21 June 1717, he takes a boat to the ports on Long Island Sound, and hangs about for a week, selling rum in quantities as small as five gallons, and leaving some with his brother-in-law to sell for a commission of one quart out of each gallon.

[2] Peter Faneuil, that versatile trader, sometimes exported flour to Louisbourg, got fish sent from Louisbourg to the French West Indies, and rum back thence to Boston; at other times he imported rum from Louisbourg. See his Letter-Book in the New England H. and G.S.

[3] Messrs. Brown of Providence had very miscellaneous dealings of this kind with Messrs. Starbuck of Nantucket. (See their correspondence of 1760–8 in the Brown MSS., J.C.B.L.)

than in the other two ports; this is not surprising, since Boston was the port of origin and if there had been no discrepancy of price the trade would not have been worth pursuing. Nevertheless, more than once the price was absolutely higher (even in the somewhat more valuable Massachusetts currency) at Boston than at the other two ports. Sometimes, as in 1757, this can be explained by military operations based on Massachusetts which raised the local demand for rum; but on other occasions no such explanation is possible. Lastly, New England rum was persistently at a premium in New York, compared both with Boston and with Philadelphia. Probably this is explained by the demand for rum in the fur trade, perhaps also, in part, by the relative insignificance of the New York distilleries. This fact also affected the price of molasses, though rather less markedly.[1]

Perhaps some idea of the confusion and the multiplicity of these exchanges can be obtained from a picture of the transactions of Gerard G. Beekman of New York, whose letter-book for the years 1752 to 1767 has been preserved in the New York Historical Society. (It may have been no accident that such a speculator was situated in New York, a port in the middle of the commercially active coast-line, with brisk privateers who brought in prize goods in war-time.[2]) At first his business might be described as normal—that is to say, he had some ventures of his own to the West Indies, and supplemented them by importing rum and molasses (apparently on his own account) from Rhode Island. In July 1753 he was selling limes and indigo on commission for Townsend White of Philadelphia; he would not, however, import indigo on his own account, as he had been offered a parcel which had arrived in New York via Jamaica and Bermuda. However, he ordered some ginger from Philadelphia (for which he paid by shipping logwood,

---

[1] Arthur H. Cole, *Wholesale Commodity Prices in the United States, 1700–1861, Statistical Supplement*, pp. 31–70.

[2] 'Cotton Coffee Sugars and Indigo are all at a stand, from the great expectation of large supply's from the prizes at York, wch the people here imagine will be a means of reducing the price of those articles considerably, but in my opinion those who have their Expectations much rais'd will be a little mistaken as the present value of them will almost admitt of their being shipt to Forreign Marketts.' (Henry Lloyd, Boston, to Aaron Lopez, Newport, 4 October 1756, Letters of Boston Merchants, 1732–1766, at Boston Public Library, MS. I, 1.1.1.)

another West India commodity) and, in the next month, bought 10,000 lb. of ginger at New London, most of which he had sold for him at Boston or Rhode Island. In March of the next year he was dealing largely in cocoa, prepared to send it to Philadelphia if it was dear there or to buy it there for importation to New York if it was cheap; finally (in May) he instructed Townsend White to buy some and send it to Boston. All this time he was selling rum on commission for a Rhode Island merchant; and, just as he was ready to exchange one West India commodity against another, so he was equally ready to exchange one kind of provisions suitable for export to the West Indies against another: he asked his correspondent in Rhode Island to send him Indian corn, and a few days later sent him bread and flour, for which the demand was just then keen in the islands.

This sort of thing went on all the time; and in the war it was diversified and stimulated by dealings in prize goods, by irregular imports of West India goods from the French islands (Beekman was interested, at one time, in seven flag-of-truce vessels) and by the demand of the various armed forces for rum. Sometimes Beekman was the agent, more often the principal. Most of his ventures seem to have been small: he was no merchant prince like John Watts, who ordered 15,000 gallons of molasses round from Rhode Island to Quebec, paying sterling bills for them in New York at a fixed price.[1] We cannot know whether Beekman's speculations enriched him, for he often lost money by them. But they must have contributed to the well-being of North America by distributing the West India commodities to the consumers and by evening the prices between one port and another.

III. THE WEST INDIA TRADE AND THE FORMATION OF CAPITAL

In countless ways West India goods and the West India trades helped to keep the wheels of American commerce turning; but it is less easy to be sure how much they contributed to the formation of American capital. Very few of the great

[1] John Watts to Nicholas Brown and Co., 29 May, 3 July, 17 July 1769, 16 July 1770, Brown MSS., J.C.B.L.

M

mercantile fortunes were built up without the help of the West
India trade; but none that I can remember was built up by it
alone before the Revolution. The most obvious contribution it
made was that of clearing the debts which North America
owed to Great Britain for consumer-goods, and so enabling the
importers of those goods to use part of the money they received
from their up-country customers as the foundation for fresh
enterprises. But this contribution can be overrated. 'Returns
via the West Indies' were not quite so easy as they were believed
to be; and, although small men and beginners may have relied
on them exclusively, big men do not even seem to have relied
on them mainly. Nicholas Brown and Aaron Lopez of Rhode
Island both incurred large debts—five or ten thousand pounds
—for dry goods to British merchants after the Peace of Paris.
Both made West India remittances—Brown in Surinam bills,
Lopez in Jamaica bills and in miscellaneous West India commodities such as logwood and mahogany. But neither relied
on these alone; their main remittances were the produce of
North America. The Browns, being furnace-masters, were
lucky to be able to send pig-iron as well as whale oil. Lopez had
more difficulty: he made some unfortunate experiments with
lumber and ships for sale before he too settled down to oil; even
so, he could not have discharged the debt without the help of
Henry Cruger, a New York merchant who does not seem to
have had strong West India connexions.[1]

The history of Aaron Lopez was instructive. In 1765 he
owed £10,000 to Cruger's son, a merchant of Bristol; for three
years the debt hardly lessened at all, and it took four or five
more to extinguish it entirely. Even so, he was building up an
even larger debt to Hayley and Hopkins, a London merchant
house to whom he transferred his custom: in 1774 he owed them
at least £12,000. All this while he carried on an extensive and
multifarious business, not least in the West Indies: he owned
several ships, including at least one in the trade between
Jamaica and London. Young Cruger called out piteously for
the reduction of his debt, which represented goods bought on

---

[1] James B. Hedges, *The Browns of Providence Plantations*, chapter 8; see also the
letters of Henry Cruger, Jr., to Aaron Lopez from 4 September 1675 onwards, in
Commerce of Rhode Island, i, 117 *et seq.*

credit from manufacturers and tradesmen who were dunning him. Lopez, to do him justice, made some attempts at reducing it, of which the most important was a scheme for remitting bills from Jamaica: this failed because his agent could not collect his debts. But Lopez could not bring himself to close down any branch of his business in order to square the account; he aimed at paying off Cruger incidentally, while keeping all his own wheels turning round. Finally Cruger exclaimed in despair, 'do in your turn take a little to yourself, by paying me my present Ballance in a *direct* way, even tho' this Mode may interfere with some favorite Plan you may have adopted'.[1] It is clear that Cruger's £10,000 and then Hayley and Hopkins's £12,000 were the financial foundation of all Lopez's enterprises. His West India business did not support his other business but was rather supported by it. The English capitalist was less directly useful to the trade between the continent and the sugar islands, and above all he had less control over it, than in the early days; but the North American entrepreneur would have been hard put to it to do without him.

This is not to say that every North American merchant who dealt with the West Indies was trading on British capital. Many of them, such as the Pepperrells of Piscataqua, Timothy Orne of Salem, and G. G. Beekman of New York, clearly were doing no such thing. These were mostly the smaller men; at least, they imported few goods from Europe, so that the chief cause of indebtedness to British capitalists did not affect them. In their hands the West India business made an original and independent contribution to the formation of American capital. But we cannot identify that contribution. They were jacks of all trades, and few of them kept accounts which show distinctly the profits from any one branch of trade or the uses to which those profits were put. We must be satisfied with the knowledge that more North American shipping was employed in this trade than in any other, that every North American port and nearly every North American merchant had something to do with it.

[1] Henry Cruger, Jr., to Aaron Lopez, 10 November 1770, *ibid*, i, 351.

INDEX